Liv

RIGHTS

Living

RIGHTSIDE

DEBBIE MORRIS
AND FRIENDS

GATEWAY
CREATE
PUBLISHING

LIVING RIGHTSIDE UP by Debbie Morris and Friends

Published by Gateway Create Publishing
Gateway Create Publishing
700 Blessed Way
Southlake, TX 76092
www.gatewaycreate.com

www.zondervan.com The "NIV" and "New International Version" are trademarks registered in the United States Patent and Trademark Office by Biblica, Inc.™

Scripture quotations marked NLT are from the Holy Bible, New Living Translation, copyright © 1996, 2004, 2007. Used by permission of Tyndale House Publishers, Inc., Wheaton, IL 60189. All rights reserved.

Scripture quotations marked THE MESSAGE are from *The Message: The Bible in Contemporary English*, copyright © 1993, 1994, 1995, 1996, 2000, 2001, 2002. Used by permission of NavPress Publishing Group.

Scripture quotations marked THE VOICE are taken from The Voice™. Copyright © 2008 by Ecclesia Bible Society. Used by permission. All rights reserved.

Cover Designers: Micah Kandras and Justin Evans
Author Photo Photographer: Corey Hale
Author Photo Makeup: Heather Spivey and Meaghan Cobb
Project Coordinator: Marsia Van Wormer
Collaborative Writer: S. George Thomas

International Standard Book Number: 978-1-62998-019-5

While the author has made every effort to provide accurate Internet addresses at the time of publication, neither the publisher nor the author assumes any responsibility for errors or for changes that occur after publication.

14 15 16 17 18 — 9 8 7 6 5 4 3 2
Printed in the United States of America

Gateway Create gratefully acknowledges the partnership of Charisma House in distributing this book.

Contents

FOREWORD

*D*o you ever wonder: What's the point of it all? Does my life really matter?

It's easy to get bogged down in the monotonous routine of daily life and fail to see there's a far greater story happening all around us. But did you know that every single day of your life a page of your story is written? You can either choose to write the story on your own, or you can surrender your pen to God and let *Him* be the Author of your story.

I know so many people who take the amazing script God has planned for their lives and turn it facedown on a table...it's upside down. Each day these people pick up a new page and try to re-create their own version of God's amazing story. But all they end up producing is a cheap knockoff.

I don't know about you, but I'm fed up with watching women (and men) settle for a subpar story. I believe, with all my heart, it's time to flip the script of your story and let the pages that once faced down—that no one could see—face the light!

It's time to start living life rightside up. After all, that's how God always intended it.

My wife, Debbie, along with a group of incredible anointed women who are her dear friends as well as invaluable members of our team at Gateway Church, wrote this book to help you see yourself the way God sees you so you can begin living out the story He has planned for you.

These women have experienced seasons of tears and seasons of laughter, times of waiting and times of receiving, days of adversity and disappointment and days of blessings and unspeakable joy. They know life isn't always easy and smooth, but they also know it's far more difficult when you try to navigate through the obstacles without God as your guide. And their stories illustrate how God always woos us back to Him when we try to strike out on our own and blaze a path without Him.

Because life is a journey, we never get to the place where we've "arrived" and know all there is to know. All along the way we learn and grow as we submit our stories to God's hand and allow Him to shape us into the bearers of His image He intended for us to be. It's a continual lifelong process…day by day by day. Even though I've been following Jesus for more than thirty years and serving in ministry for much of that time, God is constantly at work reshaping my heart to look more like His. And I know firsthand how often God uses the insights and lessons He's taught others (such as my discerning wife) to challenge and teach me in ways I'd have never discovered on my own.

God never intended for you to go at it alone either. He brings people into our lives to teach us so we can draw closer to Him, become more like Him, and then share with others the story of what He's doing in our lives. I know these eight women who've poured out their hearts in this book have personally walked out these lessons in their lives...and now *you* get the benefit of discovering those lessons firsthand as they share what God has shown them through the highs, the lows, the mundane, and everything in between.

Living Rightside Up is not just another "how-to" book. In each chapter of this book God's truths shine through so clearly and vividly that I believe you'll be challenged, encouraged, and inspired to seek out His will for your life as your story unfolds each day.

In 2 Samuel 22:25 David says: "God rewrote the text of my life when I opened the book of my heart to his eyes" (The Message). I encourage you to stop trying to write your own story. Surrender your pen to God's hand, and let Him take the mistakes and failures of your life and transform them into testimonies of His amazing grace and His unfailing goodness.

I also encourage you to open up your heart to whatever the Holy Spirit wants to teach you through the stories and truths you'll encounter in the pages of this book. I pray that, as you read this book, the Holy Spirit will show you areas of your life where you need to step back and let Him take control of your story. When you allow *Him* to rewrite the script of your life, you'll discover His purpose for your story is far greater than you could possibly imagine!

—ROBERT MORRIS
SENIOR PASTOR, GATEWAY CHURCH

Section 1

FLIPPING THE SCRIPT OF YOUR STORY

*E*VERY DAY, FROM the instant we wake up to the moment we fall asleep, we're bombarded by voices telling us who we need to be, how we need to look, why we need to change, and what we need to do better. Glamorous models with impossibly perfect bodies plastered across the covers of glossy magazines in the grocery aisle, blogs about the latest and greatest weight-loss tricks, Pinterest pins, reality TV shows, Instagram pics, romantic comedies on the big screen, Facebook posts, self-help books—they all seductively whisper to women one message: *This is what your story should look like.*

It's time to shut down the voices. It's time to start swimming against the current. It's time to flip the script. It's time to start living life rightside up.

You can stop trying to live out the story others are trying to get you to write. *Living Rightside Up* strips away the counterfeit lies we've bought into and gets to the heart of the issue—*God* is the only qualified author to write your story. And *you* are the pen and ink He's using to compose the words of a beautiful and epic poem that began the moment you drew your first breath.

In this book we expose some of the most destructive lies assaulting women today and challenge you to start seeing yourself the way God sees you. We show you practical ways to:

- Align your thoughts with God's thoughts

- Live guilt free

- Tap into the power of choice

- Rise above adversities

- Successfully resolve conflict

- Grow in seasons of waiting

- Develop a proper perspective

- Overcome the comparison trap

- And much more!

College student, career woman, stay-at-home mom, retiree, empty nester—regardless of what stage you are in life, it is never too late to flip the script of your story and start to truly live as the courageous, free, confident, exquisitely unique daughter of God He designed you to be!

Introduction

BEFORE WE BEGIN...

Debbie Morris

"Child," said the Lion, "I am telling you your story,
not hers. No one is told any story but their own."[1]
C. S. LEWIS

LIVING RIGHTSIDE UP is all about rewriting. No, not rewriting some high school essay, but rewriting the script of your life. Before you were ever conceived in your mother's womb, you were loved...even if the situations of your life haven't conveyed this message. God has loved you. He has been pursuing your heart and attention. He is and has been attentive to you. And the truth is, He is keenly aware of *every* detail in your life (even down to the exact number of hairs you color and pretend are natural).

But even after we accept that God has a plan for us and we embrace His gracious invitation to be His child, we often see weaknesses in ourselves that taunt us and seek to rob us of the joy God intended us to walk in.

The truth is, everything we think about ourselves is *not* the truth. None of us see ourselves the way God sees us. We all need to be reminded that we're so much more than what we see in the mirror.

The reason it's so important for you to grasp this truth is because you are writing a manuscript with your life that's more than a history book, more than a self-help book, more than a secret diary (in fact, it's actually being read publicly by everyone you meet). It is an incredible love story.

Living Rightside Up is about reorienting ourselves. When my husband, Robert, and I first moved to the Dallas/Fort Worth area as newlyweds, we didn't have many friends. So when we were invited to dinner at the home of a couple we'd recently become friends with, we were beyond excited.

The other woman and I talked on the phone and arranged a date and time for our dinner. Then she proceeded to give me directions. Although I'm usually pretty good with directions, she began rattling instructions on how to get around her native hometown so quickly that my hand had a hard time keeping up. (This was light-years before we had maps on our smartphones.) I *thought* I understood all the directions at the time, but the evening of our dinner proved me wrong. Robert and I got in the car with my hastily scribbled directions...which only got us to the third turn.

Frustration escalated between us as we tried to decipher my map. Admitting we couldn't get to where we needed to go with the instructions we had, Robert was forced to do what no man *ever* wants to do. He had to find a pay phone (yes, this all happened even before mobile devices were around) and call for more accurate and detailed directions.

This is how so many women I know feel. We know God has a plan for us and know a few of the steps we need to take to accomplish that plan, but we still find ourselves so often frustrated. But this is what we've learned: *we have to consciously stop each day and ask the One who knows the way what He has planned for our individual stories.*

I invite you to join me and several of my good friends on an honest and vulnerable journey as we expose some of the most destructive lies assaulting women today and challenge you (along with ourselves) to start seeing yourself the way God sees you.

Over the next several chapters we want to unpack some highly effective, real-world principles that are rooted in God's Word, so you can start living out your story as the courageous, free, confident, exquisitely unique daughter of God He designed you to be!

My desire is to encourage, inspire, and give you practical tools so you'll learn how to stop listening to the voices surrounding you and start swimming against the current. This is why I asked seven of my good friends to come alongside me and share some of the life-changing truths the Holy Spirit has been speaking to *our* hearts.

Day in and day out these seven women work alongside me, live life with me, do ministry with me, and help me lead Pink, the women's ministry of Gateway Church. These amazing ladies lead groups, oversee events, and plan massive conferences while conveying my heart and executing our shared vision not only for the women of Gateway but also for women around the world. And collectively my friends and I have learned lessons—by studying God's Word, by living through our own painful experiences, and by receiving sweet revelations from the Holy Spirit—that we believe will assist you in reaching your destination of living out your God-given dreams. Our hope is that these lessons we've learned along the way and are going to share with you in this book will be road signs that help you turn your upside down rightside up.

Just so you know exactly what you're getting with this book, I want to explain the format up front. It's not often you'll find a book with eight different contributors collaborating together, and that's what makes *Living Rightside Up* so unique. Each author is distinct in her clothing and communication style, age, and background, as well as her perspective and life experience. We hope that each unique chapter resonates in your heart.

In the pages to come you'll read stories and life lessons from myself and seven other wonderful, godly ladies. I start off the book with the first five chapters. In these opening chapters I'm going to lay the foundation for the rest of the book, because I so deeply believe that *our identity determines our destiny*. In other words, you and I have to first understand who God has created us to be before we can walk in the fullness of His calling.

After we've laid that foundation together, I'll introduce each new topic and share a little bit about my friendship with the author of that section. Some sections have one chapter; other sections may have three, four, or even five chapters. Each chapter starts off with a quote related to the message of that particular chapter. But just because we include a quote from someone doesn't mean we're endorsing that woman or man. We believe truth is truth, regardless of who gives it voice. We know God can use anyone or anything to be the mouthpiece for His truth.

You'll probably notice that most of the chapters are fairly short. We intentionally wrote this book that way, because we wanted to give you the chance to absorb the truths in easily digestible and readily applicable nuggets.

We hope you enjoy going on this journey with us! But before we begin, may I ask you to do something? Will you pray a prayer with me right now?

> *Dear Father, I ask You to open my heart as I read these words. Show me whatever it is that*

You want to show me through the pages of this book. In Jesus's name. Amen.

Let me ask you to consider doing one more thing. More than anything, we want you to hear what the Holy Spirit is speaking to you through the words we've written. What *He* has to say is far more important than what *we* have to say.

So as you finish reading each chapter, I encourage you to set the book aside for a few minutes and ask the Holy Spirit what He wants to say to you about what you've just read. And then wait and listen for His voice.

If you're willing to do that, I know beyond the shadow of a doubt that you're going to be blessed by this book as the Holy Spirit reveals His truths to you. Now, I invite you to join me as we begin our journey.

Chapter One

BLANK PAGE

Debbie Morris

Tomorrow is a blank page in the story
of your life. Decide tonight how you
will make it worth reading.[1]
KAREN KINGSBURY

CAN YOU SEE yourself sitting down with a blank canvas of white paper before you as you prepare to pen your story? Like it or not, you are writing your story. And whether it's a masterpiece hinges on your decision to either do it with the help of the Master or do it yourself.

I like to imagine myself writing in a bungalow with expansive windows overlooking waves pounding on windswept mounds of white sand. I personally prefer to write on a computer, not because I'm super tech savvy, but simply because of all the auto-correct tools.

But this isn't all about me; it's about you and your masterpiece. You can choose to use a pen or pencil if you prefer, and you get to decide what setting you'd like to be in.

Not that any of those details really matter for any of us. The story you are writing with your life is already in progress. It began before you were aware that you were scripting a manuscript, and each day you have a blank page in front of you.

Oh, the adventures you'll have, the mountains you'll climb, the victories you'll win, the obstacles you'll overcome, the fun you'll have, and the friends you'll meet. But I should warn you: it won't always be easy because there is an enemy who is determined to destroy you, people who oppose you, and an unfair playing field.

And if that weren't enough, your greatest obstacle is often yourself. If there seems to be something between you and the life you want with God—hurdles and roadblocks hindering your process—you just might be hindering yourself. At least that's what my friends and I have learned.

If you could, you might like to toss pages of your story in the trash. You know, those days that are embarrassing or too painful or even too boring. I have plenty of embarrassing stories and know that feeling all too well. Adults are supposed to know how to walk, right? Although I *am* an adult, sometimes high heels and I don't always work well together.

Recently Robert and I were given tickets to a Dallas

Cowboys' game. As an added bonus, we were also given great parking tickets (which are almost as valuable as the tickets themselves). We arrived just after kickoff, and hurrying to get inside, Robert set a pace for us that was faster than I would have preferred. You see, out of vanity's sake I had chosen to wear high heels. Are you seeing where this going? If you can already picture me sprawled out in front of the stadium, you'd be 100 percent correct. That day I learned my husband doesn't think high heels are nearly as attractive as I do. (Although I think the fact that they were the downfall of the disheveled wreckage he had to untangle and accompany into the stadium might have a little something to do with it.)

Maybe you'd like to toss chapters of pain from your story—the kind of pain that exhausts all tears, days full anguish. It hurts just to recall. All of us would like to rewrite those days. I remember the day my mom called me, not to say hi or check on me, but rather to tell me my dad had been in a horrible tractor accident. His advancement to heaven was not welcomed on my end. It pained me to be so far away that I couldn't console my mom with a hug.

I understand wanting to get rid of the pain in your life, and I dearly wish I could tell you there was a way to erase your pain and create another scenario with a happier outcome. Your story probably has some similarities with others, but yours is unique to you. The engine of time clogs away with historical moments we all share, but your story is about you and love. That's right...love.

No, not the kind that a man, woman, or even a dog can provide, but a love so amazing that it is impossible to describe. God loves you as messy as you can be. God loves you regardless. He won't stop loving you. He loved you enough to pursue you even when you were clueless. It is impossible to flip the script of your life without embracing His love.

I've been involved in ministry for thirty-three years alongside my husband and have been hands-on in women's ministry for about eighteen years. During that time we've met many people who want to rewrite the script of their lives. They want a healthy self-image, peace, contentment, joy, health, and love. Can you believe very few people tell us they want a life spiraling out of control, with heartache, selfishness, and bitterness?

So where do we start? That's a great question! Well, it's like the maps at amusement parks or malls that have a big arrow pointing out where you are in relation to the map along with the words "You Are Here." Start where you are. There is a crisp, clean sheet of paper in front you that no one has ever written on. It is yours to write a beautiful love story.

Next, decide where you want to go. Are you going with the crowd in a mindless pursuit of empty acceptance? Are you going to follow the path of family members down a twisted path of addictions? Or are you going to hear the voice of the One who loves you and follow Him?

To rewrite or redirect takes some thought. It requires purposing and focusing our thoughts and affections. We don't just stumble into the life we dreamed of. It requires some effort, just like marriage. I have been married a long time, and I now enjoy a healthy, fulfilling relationship with my high school sweetheart, but it didn't just happen overnight. Believe me. We've had struggles and conflict, but we continued to pursue each other. And the good news for you is the Lover of your soul has been pursuing you, and according to His Word, He is a rewarder of anyone who seeks Him.[2]

I hate to harp on this, but there is a clean sheet in front you. Do you see all that empty space on the page?

Someone is calling you, romancing you, and pursuing you. I dare you to answer His call.

Chapter Two

MASTERPIECE

Debbie Morris

> You don't have to be like all the others. You
> don't have to compare yourself with all
> the rest, because you're such a masterpiece,
> uniquely made, the only one like you.[1]
> STEVEN CURTIS CHAPMAN

*D*O YOU EVER look at yourself in the mirror, right after you've just woken up, and think, "Wow, I'm not just good, I am *very* good!"

Probably not, huh? If you're anything like me, you avoid turning the lights on in your bedroom or bathroom when you first wake up, because you're afraid you might see a bleary-eyed zombie staring back at you in the mirror.

As women, we so often struggle with how we view ourselves. We struggle with feeling like we're not enough.

Did you know Americans spend more than thirty *billion* dollars on beauty products every year?[2] That's a tremendous amount of money. In fact, it's more than the annual GDP of several nations, including Mongolia, Zimbabwe, Madagascar, and Armenia. Just on beauty products alone.

Did you also know that there are more than 240,000 self-help books on Amazon.com right now?[3] That's a ton of information, right at our fingertips, just to improve ourselves. But even with *all* of that, so many of us still struggle with really knowing who we are and feeling comfortable in our own skin.

I can relate. Through the years I've grown more and more comfortable with myself...at least until I get put in new and unfamiliar territory. Because Robert had agreed to participate in a banquet where President George W. Bush was the keynote speaker, we were afforded the honor to "hang out" in the green room with him.

Knowing this event was soon coming up, I asked a friend with a gift in fashion to assist me in choosing my clothing. The day before the event we met and selected an outfit that was perfect. But as I got dressed on the big day, I realized I wouldn't be able to wear the shoes all night long. Because I knew my friend would find out I hadn't worn the "perfect shoes" she picked out and instead opted for my old suede boots, I called her to give her a heads up about my plan.

As you might guess, she would not hear of it. She

picked up another pair of shoes and met me at the banquet. I ended up changing my shoes in the parking lot with several men waiting to escort us to the waiting room. I wish you could have seen how funny this all was to me. But it gets even funnier.

When I started walking through the enormous lobby in my new perfect shoes, I kept stepping out of them. Before we made it to the elevator, Robert looked at me and said, "Go change shoes. You look ridiculous!" So the entire entourage of men followed me back to the car so I could change my shoes again. On our way back through the lobby, one of the people working at the banquet actually made a comment about how I seemed to be walking much better. So I wore my black suede boots to the banquet where I met the president. Years ago I would have been too embarrassed to go in my boots, but instead I decided to make the best of it by being happy and having happy feet!

But why do you think so many of us have such a difficult time embracing who we are? I believe it's because our self-image is skewed.

So what's the *right* way for us to view ourselves? In order to start rewriting the script of our lives, we have to first get an accurate perspective by going back to the very first woman and man. We need to sift through the pages of history and take a look at the original mold God created and learn some things that will change what we see, what we hear, and what we do. And over the next several chapters that is exactly what we're going to do together. So, "let's start at the very beginning," because that's "a very good place to start."

The first eleven chapters of the Book of Genesis give us the *beginning* of our story. They set the stage for the rest of the Bible and all of history. Genesis tells us that when God spoke, He created life. With enormous creativity He spoke, and light came about. Isn't that amazing? Just by *speaking*, God creates. He speaks, and water begins to move and separate huge masses of land.

God didn't need apps like Pinterest. He didn't need Houzz. He didn't need any kind of help to come up with the most mind-blowingly creative ideas. From the reservoir of who He was, He created the most amazing things with just His words.

There are so many times when I wish I had that same power. Wouldn't you just love to give a command and see it immediately happen? When I was a young mom with three little kids, I quickly learned that I don't have quite the same ability to speak and instantly bring order to chaos. Believe me, I tried! I'd tell my kids, "Children, let your rooms be clean!" And then I'd wait for them to instantly jump up and obey. To my disappointment, nothing ever happened.

But here's what's so fascinating to me. Even though God *does* have the ability to speak and make anything instantly come into being, He didn't use that particular power to create us. Instead of speaking us into existence, He chose to get much more intimately involved in our creation.

In the original language the Bible tells us that God scooped dirt from the ground, sculpted it into a human-like shape and created man, and then He breathed life into him. But even though God Himself created Adam, He didn't create him to be self-sufficient. Up to this point God has looked at everything He's made and declared that it was good. Now, God looks at Adam and says: "It is *not good* for the man to be alone."[4]

So God put Adam to sleep, and He "fashioned into a woman" a rib from Adam's body.[5] I love that word *fashioned*. I get such an image of intentionality from that word, and I love the thought that God deliberately took a little more time on us.

Imagine the most skillful master painter in the world—better than even Michelangelo, Monet, Van Gogh, Rembrandt, Da Vinci, or any of the other great artists in history—sitting down before an untouched canvas to create his *magnum opus*—his final and finest masterpiece. That's us, ladies! With His own hands God crafted and "created mankind in his own image, in the image of God he created them; male and female he created them."[6] And when He was finished, He looked at His creation and said, "Oh, this is *very* good!"

I'd also like to point out that God made a point of telling us He created *both male and female* in His image. Both genders are required to wholly reflect the image of God. That means God has *both masculine and feminine characteristics*. While, yes, Jesus came to earth in the form of a man, and throughout the Bible the Father, Son, and Holy Spirit are referred to in the masculine sense, don't make the mistake of thinking that God is male.

The Bible is very clear that God is spirit, and as spirit He isn't limited to gender.[7] Just because we call God Father doesn't mean He's "male." It means He cares for, protects, disciplines, and loves us as the very best father would—only God is infinitely better. In the same way, when the Bible refers to God as being our husband, it's saying that God loves and protects His relationship with us as a good husband would.

When we read the Bible, we often see the masculine pronouns "He," "Him," and "His" used to refer to God; He is never referred to by a feminine pronoun like "she" or "her." However, that doesn't mean God is male. Just as the word *mankind* encompasses both men and women, masculine pronouns referring to God don't negate the fact that His image is reflected in both men and women.

In fact, throughout the Bible, we also see Him described with feminine metaphors:[8]

+ God is like a mother eagle hovering over her young (Deut. 32:11).

+ God cares for His people as a midwife cares for a newborn child (Ps. 22:9–10; 71:6, Isa. 66:9).

- As a mother would never forget her child, God never forgets His children (Isa. 49:15).

- God comforts like a mother comforting her child (Isa. 66:13).

What's more, the Bible describes the Holy Spirit as having several attributes that culture typically defines as more feminine qualities—Comforter, Counselor, Helper, Advocate, Strengthener.

Now you may be wondering: "Why do we have to spend so much time on this?" It's because you have an enemy who is out to hide and twist the truth so you'll buy into a lie and live out a tragically mediocre story. Understanding where we came from *matters*, because our identity cannot be separated from our origin. Out of everything else in creation—the birds, the fish, the animals that live on land, the plants and trees—you and I are wholly unique, because God personally designed us. That's why He doesn't want us to live day to day, just surviving—He wants us to have an abundant life.

Here's the bottom-line truth: you can never truly know who *you* are until you know who *God* is. Why? Because as a woman, you were created in God's likeness. It is absolutely vital you not only *understand* that truth but also *receive* that truth.

Can you imagine how amazing it would be to view yourself the way that God views you—as His priceless masterpiece? There was a time when the birds sang, the flowers bloomed, and humans had a healthy self-image. The Bible tells us: "In those days the man and his wife were both naked and were not ashamed."[9] They had a healthy self-image. They weren't hiding. They were unashamed.

So what went wrong?

Chapter Three

FOCUS

Debbie Morris

Choose to view life through God's eyes. This
will not be easy because it doesn't come naturally
to us. We cannot do this on our own. We have
to allow God to elevate our vantage point.[1]
CHARLES SWINDOLL

EVERYTHING WAS PERFECT in the Garden of Eden—
not just good or really good or even great...but perfect.
I don't think we truly have the capacity to comprehend
what it must have been like to live in a perfect world, to
have a perfect relationship.

We look around us, and all we see is brokenness—
from the news we see on TV to the hurts and wounds
we experience in our hearts. Deep down, each of us
knows the world is broken. It doesn't work quite right.

And we long for things to be fixed, to be made whole, to work the way they're supposed to.

Once upon a time—as hard as it may be to imagine—life was perfect. But then, in an instant, everything changed. The Book of Genesis tells us how it all went down (literally):

> Now the serpent was more crafty than any of the wild animals the Lord God had made. He said to the woman, "Did God really say, 'You must not eat from any tree in the garden'?"
>
> The woman said to the serpent, "We may eat fruit from the trees in the garden, but God did say, 'You must not eat fruit from the tree that is in the middle of the garden, and you must not touch it, or you will die.'"
>
> "You will not certainly die," the serpent said to the woman. "For God knows that when you eat from it your eyes will be opened, and you will be like God, knowing good and evil."
>
> When the woman _saw that the fruit of the tree was good for food and pleasing to the eye_, and also desirable for gaining wisdom, she took some and ate it. She also gave some to her husband, who was with her, and he ate it. Then the eyes of both of them were opened, and they realized they were naked; so they sewed fig leaves together and made coverings for themselves.[2]

One question led to a conversation. One conversation led to a look. One look led to a touch. One touch led to a bite. One bite led to death.

Now, we don't know if Eve or Adam had ever secretly entertained the idea of eating the fruit before this moment. But based on what we do know, deciding to eat the fruit wasn't a long, elaborate process. Eve listened to the serpent, and then did you notice what she did next? She *looked* at the fruit, and it looked good to her.

Like Eve, each of us takes in and evaluates information through the portals of our eyes. The problem is our eyes don't always give us the whole picture. Sure, the fruit *looked good* to Eve, but it definitely wasn't *good for her*...or for anyone since.

We can't always trust what we see with our own eyes. They don't give us an accurate reading of things. We look at the world through the filter of our eyes and end up constantly comparing ourselves to others—whether it's our abilities, weight, hair color, status, or gifts. When we do this, though, we end up either falling into a pit of superiority or a pit of inferiority.

When we're comparing ourselves with someone or something else, we're looking at the wrong thing. We're trying to measure ourselves. But because of Eve and Adam's choice to disobey God in the garden, we don't even have a clear understanding of *who* we are. In his second letter to the believers in Corinth Paul wrote: "For we would never dare to compare ourselves with people who have based their worth on self-commendation. They check themselves against and compare themselves with one another. It just shows that they don't have any sense!"[3] When it comes to our own self-perception, our eyes tend to lie to us and distort the truth—we have myopia.

Myopia (commonly known as nearsightedness or shortsightedness) is an eye condition that afflicts roughly 34 million people in the United States and anywhere from 800 million to 2.3 billion people around the world.[4] Someone who has myopia sees people and objects that aren't directly in front of her face as blurry and out of focus. And the only way someone with myopia can see correctly is either by placing a lens directly in front of her eyes (glasses or contacts) or through surgery.

I used to be one of those 800 million plus people who wore contacts and glasses. (I hope no one *ever* unearths my old school pictures with some extremely dorky glasses.) Several years ago I finally became brave enough to have Lasik surgery performed. And let me tell you, it was amazing! On the way to the doctor's office I could hardly see anything. Immediately after the surgery I looked out the doctor's office window and could see things more clearly than I could ever remember. As my eyes healed from the procedure, my vision continued to steadily improve. However, there was a small tradeoff for a life without contacts. As I had been warned before, I ended up losing some of my ability to see fine details up close.

When Adam and Eve ate from the tree of the knowledge of good and evil, sin entered the world, and everything changed. "Then the eyes of both of them were opened, and they realized they were naked."[5] This is the exact moment when poor self-image was birthed in the human race. Sure, their eyes were opened, but they opened in such a way that they would never see as clearly again. Everything they looked at now was filtered through their myopia, and as a result, a paralyzing awareness of what they were *not* was born.

Up to this point they'd never experienced even the tiniest bit of shame. They were completely naked and never once questioned it or even thought about it. All they knew was God had created them this way, and it was good. After disobeying God's command, though, they suddenly looked at themselves and felt an overwhelming sense of shame and insecurity. So Adam and Eve physically did what most of us emotionally do when we feel shame—they covered themselves with whatever they could find so that they wouldn't have to feel exposed and vulnerable in front of each other or in front of God.

But thankfully the story doesn't end there. God came looking for them.

> Then the man and his wife heard the sound of the Lord God as he was walking in the garden in the cool of the day, and they hid from the Lord God among the trees of the

garden. But the LORD God called to the man, "Where are you?"

[Adam] answered, "I heard you in the garden, and *I was afraid* because I was naked; so I hid."

And [God] said, "Who told you that you were naked? Have you eaten from the tree that I commanded you not to eat from?"[6]

Adam's response to God's question illustrates a truth that's important for us to grasp before we can view ourselves correctly: *fear is at the core of poor self-image.* When we have fear in our hearts, we simply cannot see ourselves or our circumstances clearly.

Think about it. What is self-image? It's the perception you have of yourself—how you look, who you are, what your worth is, and how valuable you are. But that perception is then projected on to how *others* see you...at least in your mind. So when you have an incorrect view of yourself (because what you see with your own eyes isn't trustworthy), you subconsciously fear that everyone else sees you the same way. And because you think people view you negatively, you hide by covering yourself up with various defense mechanisms:

+ Concealing your true thoughts and feelings because you don't want to rock the boat

- Downplaying someone else's success because it makes you feel inadequate

- Retaliating with anger when you feel hurt, threatened, or afraid

- Overcompensating by always having to *be the best* (as opposed to *doing your best*)

- Throwing yourself into a flurry of activities in an effort to avoid being still and facing your fear that you're not enough

- Shutting down your emotions and keeping people at arm's length

- Avoiding opportunities to grow, learn, and be challenged because you're afraid you don't have what it takes

And the list goes on. Have you ever done any of these things before? I'm definitely guilty. There have been countless times when I've lost sight of how God sees me and, instead, focused on what my fear was telling me. Whenever I feel like I don't quite measure up, I have a tendency to hide. The only question is: what am I going to choose to hide behind? Will it be criticizing others, becoming a workaholic, having an obsession with clothes, working out excessively, or obsessing over my kids in an unhealthy way?

Being self-aware can be a blessing when we view ourselves through the proper lens and realize our desperate need for God. But when we don't, it's a curse that leads us to question God and ourselves. We end up looking at the wrong things—such as someone else's abilities, appearance, and possessions—causing us to chase our tails and not value our God-given gifts and abilities.

I want you to grasp this truth: *you are the only person in existence who will ever be able to use* your *abilities*. If you don't use the gifts and abilities God has given you, they will be lost and wasted forever.

I—and I alone—can be God's expression of Himself in me here on earth. You—and only you—can be God's expression of Himself in you here on earth. God needs *each of us* to be our own uniquely individual expression of Him here on earth.

So how do we get past the fact that we can't rely on what we see with our own eyes? The answer is actually pretty simple (but incredibly freeing once we grasp the magnitude of it): we need to stop relying on what we see with our own eyes.

That's it? Yep.

The Bible tells us, "For we walk by faith, not by sight."[7] Or, to put it another way: "The path we walk is charted by faith, not by what we see with our eyes."[8]

OK, so let's break this down: We have to walk by faith and not by what we see. So the next question is: faith in what exactly? The answer—we have to place our faith in the fact that God is who He says He is. Well, who does God say He is?

Here are just a *few* things we know:

- God is our Father, and He always takes care of His children.[9]

- God has the power to always rescue us.[10]

- God always meets our needs.[11]

- God gives us peace that goes beyond our understanding.[12]

- God is love.[13]

So God is love, and "where God's love is, there is no fear, because God's perfect love drives out fear."[14] That means *any* area of our lives where we're experiencing fear is an area where we're not experiencing God's presence and love.

Are you experiencing fear in any area of your life? Invite the Lord to invade those areas and fill you with His presence and love. David wrote in the Psalms:

> I sought the Lord, and he answered me and delivered me from all my fears.[15]

Are you struggling to see yourself the way God sees you? Ask Him to help you see yourself in light of who He has called you to be. In his letter to the Ephesians Paul wrote:

> I ask—ask the God of our Master, Jesus Christ, the God of glory—to make you intelligent

and discerning in knowing him personally, *your eyes focused and clear, so that you can see exactly what it is he is calling you to do,* grasp the immensity of this glorious way of life he has for his followers, oh, the utter extravagance of his work in us who trust him— endless energy, boundless strength![16]

Do you feel unimportant and worthless? Do you wonder if you have any significant contribution to make? Know that God has chosen you, and you are precious to Him. The apostle Peter wrote:

As you come to him, a living stone *rejected by men but in the sight of God chosen and precious,* you yourselves like living stones are being built up as a spiritual house, to be a holy priesthood, to offer spiritual sacrifices acceptable to God through Jesus Christ. For it stands in Scripture: "Behold, I am laying in Zion a stone, *a cornerstone chosen and precious*, and whoever believes in him will not be put to shame."[17]

My prayer is that you take hold of this truth and let it transform your life: *What* you *see does not define you.* It will *never* define you.

Ever since the Garden of Eden every single child who has come into this world has been born with spiritual myopia. I'm not exempt from it. You're not exempt from it. That's why we so desperately need a new lens to see through.

And here's the lens—you are defined by what *God* sees.

Do you know what God sees when He looks at you? He sees *His daughter*. He sees a precious, valuable, beautiful, exquisite, lovely, priceless masterpiece whom He created *in His image*. Because Jesus took on your fear and your shame on the cross, it's not yours to carry any longer. You don't have to hide in fear. You don't have to cover up your "flaws" in shame any longer, because Jesus's blood covers them all.

When God looks at you, do you know what He sees?

He sees Jesus. And because He sees you *through* Jesus...you are perfect.

Chapter Four

WHAT'S IN A NAME?

Debbie Morris

Let's quit treating our history like a prophecy.
If you are in Christ, never let anybody tell you
that who you have been you will always be.[1]
BETH MOORE

WHEN YOU FIRST learn a friend is expecting a baby, what's the first question you ask her (after you're done jumping up and down and screaming for joy, of course)? You usually ask, "So, when are you due?" Or maybe, "Do you know if it's going to be a boy or a girl?" More often than not, you eventually get around to the big question: "Have you picked out any names yet?"

In *Romeo and Juliet*, Shakespeare's famous tragedy about love-struck teenagers, Juliet asks Romeo this question: "What's in a name? That which we call a rose, by any other name would smell as sweet." She's basically saying that the names we've been given are meaningless and artificial.[2] But that's not really true, is it?

Our Western culture has an almost obsessive fascination with names. If you search for "baby name" books on Amazon, more than thirty thousand results pop up.[3] There are hundreds of websites and apps designed to give you info about the origin, popularity, and meaning of just about any name you could imagine— and that's just the tiniest tip of the iceberg. In the past three years the phrase "baby names" appeared seventy-eight different times in various *New York Times* articles. Twenty years earlier? That phrase showed up only about seven times over the same time frame.[4]

Whenever someone famous has a baby, there's always fierce competition among the major media outlets to be the first one to break the big news on what the little boy or girl is going to be called. When the world found out Kate Middleton and Prince William had a new baby boy, the big question everyone seemed to be asking was, "What's his name going to be?"

A name is far more than just an arrangement of letters haphazardly thrown together. One of the very first things we teach our children is their name; they are like tags or labels that define us. As a result, our self-perceptions are usually linked with our names. They can be an anchor of our souls.

People in ancient times understood and were very conscious of the power of names. They believed there was a vital connection between the name and the person it identified. A name somehow represented the very *nature* of the person.

This means that the naming of a baby was very important in the Bible. In choosing a name, the parents could reflect the circumstances of the child's birth, their own feelings, their gratitude to God, their hopes and prayers for the child, and their commitment of the child to God. The name Isaac reflected the "laughter" of his mother at his birth.[5] Esau was named "hairy" because of his appearance, and Jacob was named "supplanter" because he grasped his brother Esau's heel.[6] Moses received his name because he was drawn out of the water.[7]

Most people presume that Eve was always called Eve, but did you know she actually received three different names? When God created man and woman and placed them in the Garden of Eden, they just had one name:

> Man and female created he them; and blessed them, and called *their* name Adam, in the day when they were created.[8]

God attentively crafted the woman *in His image* by fashioning her from one of the man's ribs. (By the way, only He could take a rib and make something so beautiful.) But God never gave the woman a different name from the man. He called them *both* Adam, which means "mankind" or "human." There was a male "Adam" and a female "Adam"—and they were one flesh.[9]

It was the man who named his counterpart "woman." When God brought the woman to the man and he saw her for the very first time, his heart skipped a beat. He was so happy and overcome with adoration, he couldn't contain himself:

> "At last!" the man exclaimed. "This one is bone from my bone, and flesh from my flesh! She will be called 'woman,' because she was taken from 'man.'"[10]

When Adam named her "woman," he was saying, "You're like me, but you're also distinctly different. You're part of me, but you're also unique." *She both complemented and completed Adam.* There was a God-given need in man that only woman could fulfill.

Isn't that what every one of us wants deep down in our hearts? To be appreciated as a priceless gift from God? To be like yet unique? To complement and complete?

In the Garden of Eden the woman experienced pure love and unabashed adoration from her husband…until they both disobeyed God by eating the fruit from the tree He had commanded them to never consume. From that moment on, sin entered the world, and their relationship with God and with each other was fractured.

The Bible tells us: "Then the man—Adam—named his wife Eve, because she would be the mother of all who live."[11] No longer would he refer to her as "bone from my bone, and flesh from my flesh." Now it was "mother of all who live." Their sweet moment was gone. Separation had entered their relationship. Adam assigned her a name separate from his own. This naming stripped away an aspect of their oneness. It was no longer about who she *was* but what she would *do*. It was like he was saying: "You're *you*. And I'm *me*."

Do you think Eve heard "shame" whenever Adam called her Eve instead of woman? I wonder if it represented separation and failure to her. And when her new life of hardship outside the perfect paradise of the garden began to rub on her, I wonder if her new name began to rub on her as well.

So why are we talking so much about names? We all already have names. Well, the reason it's so important is our names are going on the manuscripts we are writing. And our experiences often cause us to subconsciously attach an erroneous definition or belief system to our names. Once you attach that label to your name, that's always what you *hear*…until God helps you rewrite the meaning of your name. Encoded in what you hear in your name are internal triggers that attempt to override everything you do and think.

Your name might be Jessica, but every time you hear it, you feel like it means "dummy." Maybe you're Melissa, but you feel "abandoned" when you hear your name. Or perhaps you've been divorced, and whenever you hear your legal name, you hear "defeat," "failure," and "brokenness." Those internal signals are so ingrained in who we think we are it is often difficult to separate their message from the truth.

Throughout the Bible we see God changing the names of people—Abraham, Sarah, Peter, and Paul all received new names. Now, I'm not suggesting we all go out and change our legal names, but I *am* suggesting we change what we hear and think about ourselves when it comes to our names. Everyone calls me Debbie, but for years, every time I heard my name said, a voice in my head changed it to "little Debbie." As a grown-up, I felt I couldn't make adult decisions. I still felt like a child. I had unknowingly attached a label to my name that didn't reflect the truth.

I don't know what your name is, but here's what I do know: if you've been struggling with accepting yourself, you may be hearing a voice calling you by the wrong name. It's time to start listening to the right Voice:

> Whoever has ears, let them hear what the Spirit says to the churches. To the one who is victorious, I will give some of the hidden manna. I will also give that person a white stone *with a new name written on it*, known only to the one who receives it.[12]

And *you will be given a new name by the Lord's own mouth.* The LORD will hold you in his hand for all to see—a splendid crown in the hand of God. Never again will you be called "The Forsaken City" or "The Desolate Land." *Your new name will be "The City of God's Delight" and "The Bride of God," for the Lord delights in you and will claim you as his bride.*[13]

You don't have to hide in shame and fear anymore as Eve did in the garden. God has claimed you and named you—you are His "beloved," His "bride," His "delight"! And *that* is the name you want to put on your manuscript.

Chapter Five

DON'T STOP BELIEVING

Debbie Morris

Define yourself radically as one beloved
by God. This is the true self. Every
other identity is illusion.[1]
BRENNAN MANNING

$\mathcal{M}$ORE OFTEN THAN not, the first time we meet someone, the first question we ask is, "What's your name?", and that's quickly followed by, "So, what do you do?" Because, for better or for worse, what we do defines us in our own eyes and those of most people.

In the last chapter we talked about how Adam named his wife Eve, because she was "the mother of all who live."[2] While their names—man and woman—had spoken of their oneness, now he had given Eve a name that unequivocally separated her identity from his. And with this name change came a tarnished

38

self-image transferable to every woman who came after her. Eve's identity was no longer based on who *she was*; it was based on her function—on what *she did*.

Herein lies the insecurity in so many women. Although there are countless who love to be mothers, I know several who wonder, "Is this the only purpose God has for me as a woman? Is my identity only wrapped up in being a mother?"

Even if you're not a mother, a lot of times your identity gets wrapped up in what you do. Employee, boss, mother, daughter, sister, wife, grandmother, coworker— whatever title you have, all too often it becomes about what you *do* instead of who you *are*.

I've often talked with women who desperately want to stand up and loudly announce to anyone willing to listen: "Yes, I'm a wife. And yes, I'm a mother. *But that's not who I am. There's more to me than what I do!*"

It's a universal and ageless struggle. Ever since the time of Eve the human race has been striving to make a name for itself:

> Then they said, "Come, let us build ourselves a city, with a tower that reaches to the heavens, *so that we may make a name for ourselves*; otherwise we will be scattered over the face of the whole earth."
>
> But the LORD came down to see the city and the tower the people were building. The LORD said, "If as one people speaking the

same language they have begun to do this, then nothing they plan to do will be impossible for them. Come, let us go down and confuse their language so they will not understand each other."

So the LORD scattered them from there over all the earth, and they stopped building the city. That is why it was called Babel— because there the LORD confused the language of the whole world. From there the LORD scattered them over the face of the whole earth.[3]

As you can see, the desire to be recognized is nothing new. That was the people's sole motivation in building that tower. Despite all their best efforts, though, we don't find a single individual's name listed in this biblical account (or anywhere else for that matter).

Have your efforts to find self-worth and meaning ever driven you to go to great lengths to make a name for yourself? Do you worry if you don't do something to make a name for yourself, someone else will make one for you (and it might not be the one you want)?

Best-selling books, blog posts, and self-help gurus tell us: "Market yourself...build your platform...leverage your influence...that's the only way to get ahead and be recognized." And while there's nothing inherently wrong with those methods, they're not the only way to leave a lasting impact. Sometimes the best way to leave a lasting impact is to *not* make a name for yourself.

There is story after story in the Bible of nameless men and women who altered the course of history. The Book of Judges tells us about Abimelech, a son of the judge Gideon. According to the Bible, Abimelech was an unprincipled, ambitious man who often engaged in war with his own subjects and killed sixty-nine of his seventy half-brothers just so he could be the sole ruler and king over the people of Shechem. For three years Abimelech ruled as an evil tyrant until a "certain woman" defeated him by crushing his skull with a rock.[4]

Although we don't know her name, we certainly know the result of what she did. She didn't need for her name to be known to make an impact, and you know what? Neither do you! Your life matters!

What you've done in the past or what you're doing today does not have to define you. I know so many of us women who feel shame over what we do or what we've done. What makes it worse is, when you're faced with a choice to do something that's only going to cause you to beat yourself up later, the devil does his best to entice and deceive you just as he did Eve in the garden by whispering, "Oh, you can do it. It'll be OK. You can get away with doing that." Then the moment you give in and do it, the devil starts accusing you: "I can't believe you did that! Look at you. You're so awful. Nobody would like you, let alone love you, if they knew what you did."

Because his goal is to steal and destroy your

God-given identity—His beloved, His bride, His delight—the devil does everything within his power to get you caught up in focusing on what you've done and wallowing in your shame and guilt.

So what do you need to do if you're going to be a woman who is confident and resting in who your Father made you to be? (Glad you *finally* asked!) *If you want a healthy perspective of who you are, you have to believe what God says about you.*

> The people asked Jesus, "What are the things God wants us to do?" Jesus answered, "The work God wants you to do is this: *Believe the One he sent.*"[5]

That's it. Believe you are who God says you are. I know that sounds quite simplistic, but it is a revolutionary practice that leads to an extraordinary life.

God's Word instructs us to: "Put on your new nature, and be renewed as you learn to know your Creator and become like him."[6] The more you get to know God and find out what He thinks about you, the more you start looking like Him.

Do you have any idea what God thinks about you? If not, let me enlighten you. You are:

- Beautifully and wonderfully made
- Rescued from shame, sin, and death
- Free from condemnation

+ More than a conqueror

+ Called and chosen by Him

+ Complete

+ Pure and spotless before Him

+ Known by Him

+ His friend

+ His daughter

+ His beloved

+ His bride

If you blew right through that list, I want you to go back and look at each one of those individually. Read each one slowly, and really think about how it applies specifically to you. And then ask God to reveal the truth of it to you.

There is *no one* on earth who can completely define who you are by what you look like, what name you are called, or what you do. Defining you is God's job and His alone.

> For the Scripture says, "Everyone who believes
> in him will not be put to shame."[7]

Now it's *your* job to believe what your Creator says about you, to hear Him calling you His "beloved," and choose to see yourself with His eyes.

Section 2

THE TRUTH ABOUT GUILT

I'd like you to meet my friend Adana...

WOMEN TEND TO be multitaskers. We wear many different hats daily. We may be a daughter, sister, friend, wife, mom, employer, or employee. Even when we're sitting still, we're often mentally preparing for the next day, solving problems, rehearsing problems, and evaluating what we wish we'd done differently. Most of us daily surrender our lives in service for others.

In our busyness, what can happen over time is that we forget how to receive anything for ourselves. It can be something as minor as a daily shower or eating more than snacks on the run, but sometimes it can also turn into something more serious like putting aside our need to get medical checkups or creating time and space to spend time with our Father and feed ourselves spiritually or just have fun!

The busier life gets, the louder it tends to sound—and the more we begin seeing ourselves through broken filters, especially when we're constantly surrounded by "industry experts" obsessed with dispensing the latest and greatest "must-haves" for our homes, our children, and our personal and professional lives. We can quickly descend into a pit of guilt because we believe the lie that we'll never measure up—no matter what we do. And so we end up feeling ashamed and completely inadequate. Perhaps most tragically, we project our self-inflicted fears and insecurities onto God and wrongly believe He sees us through *our* filter.

Helen Keller has been quoted as saying she'd rather walk with a friend in the dark than alone in the light.[1] Adana Wilson, an able minister who quickly connects with the hearts of women, is that kind of friend. We share a love for worship, Queen Esther, and Mexican food as well as a mutual disdain for sushi. In the next couple of chapters Adana shines the beautiful bright light of truth on the guilt we *all* struggle with. She vulnerably shares her heart and exposes common feelings of inadequacy as well as our resistance to receiving. Adana paints a beautiful portrait of our adoption into the family of God, and as she illustrates how we've been *chosen*, she helps us see the way to let it go.

Chapter Six

LET IT GO!

Adana Wilson

I was tormented with guilt for years.
In fact, it was so bad that if I didn't
feel wrong, I didn't feel right![1]
JOYCE MEYER

GUILT. ONE WAY or another, we all deal with it.

I feel like I'm a terrible mom. I wish I could say I have a Pinterest-worthy schedule of fun, creative after-school activities for each day of the week, or that I plan out and prep healthy meal options for my family a month in advance. But honestly, some days I call it a success if I can just throw together something that resembles a dinner and make sure no one's rushed to the ER.

If he only knew all the things I've done wrong in the past, he'd never want to be my boyfriend. I mean, look at him! He's kind, funny, hot…he makes me feel like a princess. But that's only 'cause he doesn't know me the way I do. I'm just waiting for the other shoe to drop.

I'm a terrible Christian. I've overslept every morning this week and haven't had any time to read my Bible. And I don't even have a good excuse—it's because I've been staying up too late watching TV. Watch, I'll probably get a ticket on the way to work or get a flat tire or something. God's not going to bless me when I can't be disciplined enough to spend time with Him every morning, is He?

Doesn't guilt stink? A few years ago Bible teacher Beth Moore surveyed more than a thousand women and asked them, "What do you feel is the most difficult part about being a woman?" Do you know what one of the top answers was? That's right—guilt.[2]

There are two sides of guilt—guilt because of wrongs we've committed and guilt based on how we feel. Guilt makes us feel like we never measure up, that we're always lacking in some area. Because of guilt, we beat ourselves up over the slightest shortcomings. We feel guilt because we aren't a good friend or guilt over not making it to our coworker's baby shower.

And social media doesn't really do us any favors in the guilt area, does it? Every day we're inundated with blog posts, Facebook statuses, tweets on Twitter, Pinterest pins, and pics on Instagram of women we know (and many we don't) who seem so confident, carefree, and capable of taking on the world. And most of the time the people who post stories and images about recipes they've whipped together, projects they've crafted, romantic trips they've taken, or their daily workout regimen are genuinely well meaning. Their goal is to inspire, not shame. But so often it makes me feel "less than"—that I'm not cooking (I hate to cook), exercising, crafting, or doing enough. Can you relate at all?

God has given each of us specific strengths and talents. I know one of my strengths is "responsibility." If I'm tasked with a job to do, I *will* complete the job—no matter what. It also means every time I see something that needs to be done—regardless of whether it's my responsibility or not—I feel like I need to fix it or take care of it. The shadow side of this strength is I often find myself taking responsibility for things I shouldn't. If I'm not careful to recognize what is my responsibility and what isn't, I quickly find myself worn out and discouraged, because I'm trying to fix things I was never asked to correct and that are simply not my responsibility. My desire to help people out can lead to me being overloaded and running in ten thousand different directions.

The balance in my life comes when I evaluate a

situation to determine if it's actually my responsibility to fix. If it's not, then I ask myself, "Do I have time to fix it?" If the answer is no, then (as much as I hate to) I politely decline to take on whatever task is being asked of me. Pretty much every time I tell someone no, I battle feeling guilty. I feel like I've let her down or created a hardship for her. The truth is, there's someone else out there who could most likely complete the task and do it just as well as, if not better than, me.

You can't allow guilt or a false sense of responsibility to rope you into doing everything for everyone. God has never called or asked you to do that. Flipping the script of your story is sometimes nothing more than drawing boundaries to keep things in order and walking in the peace that saying no is often saying yes to something better!

I know so many moms who stay at home and feel guilty because they aren't contributing enough financially to their families. On the other hand, I've talked with several moms who work and feel guilty they're not at home spending more time with their kids. It's a catch-22. And then, to make matters worse, women on both sides of the spectrum judge one another (I believe out of guilt) rather than supporting and encouraging one another.

I'm a working mother of three boys, and I enjoy working. In fact, I always have. Other than a brief season, I've worked since I was sixteen years old. When my children were very young, I worked part-time or from home. But other than that, I've worked a full-time professional job for the majority of my life. As a mom, I've dealt with guilt both ways. During the season I didn't work and when I was working part-time, finances in our family were tight. Whenever I spent money—whether it was for groceries, clothes, or visits to the doctor—I'd feel guilty for not contributing more to the household financially. On the other hand, when I *was* working full-time, I'd feel guilty when my boys would come home and I wasn't there to welcome them or offer them an afternoon snack.

I wish the Bible was clear-cut one way or the other, but there isn't a Scripture verse that says, "Thou shalt work," or, "Thou shalt stay at home." While I know I have a responsibility to "train up my children in the way they should go,"[3] I also know the "model woman" described in Proverbs 31 obviously worked.

I know regardless of what choice I'd made, the devil was going to try and use guilt against me. Thankfully, in whatever season I've been in, God has given me His grace. At times it was grace to stay home and raise my children. Other times it was grace to work and still raise my children. The bottom line for me was having the peace of knowing my husband and I had prayed and were in agreement—whether it was working outside the home or working inside the home. I wasn't doing anything "wrong," and the guilty feelings that would spring up from time to time were just that—*feelings*!

Most of the women I know deal with guilty feelings

that aren't true. And I believe one of the primary reasons we as women struggle so much with feeling guilty is because we've bought into the lie that we are called to have it all and do it all. Here are some of the results of believing that lie:

+ We have too much to do.

+ We feel exhausted.

+ We constantly compare ourselves to other women who seem to have it all together.

+ We feel like we have to be perfect in every area.

+ We use unhealthy means to remove the guilty feeling (excessive shopping, exercising, working, eating, etc.).

Guilt touches *all* of us. And if left unchecked, guilt drags us down the rabbit hole of regret, shame, and self-loathing. When that happens, it's all too often debilitating—we end up paralyzed by the guilt eating away at us.

Have you ever felt that kind of guilt before? Like you just don't quite measure up to everyone else? You see others serving God and having a positive impact on the people around them, but you don't think you have what it takes for Him to use you. Mother Teresa? Billy Graham? Sure. You? Not so much.

The other side of guilt is based on wrongs we have actually committed, and we are *all* guilty of doing something wrong! There is not a woman (or man) on this earth who isn't guilty of something.

Isaiah could certainly relate. When Uzziah, the king of Israel, died, his world was suddenly thrown into a tailspin. Isaiah had grown up around the king's court, so the news of Uzziah's death left him feeling lost, confused, uncertain, and hopeless. But at this low point in Isaiah's life God appeared to him.

Isaiah writes, "In the year that King Uzziah died, I saw the Lord, high and exalted, seated on a throne." It's an awe-inspiring scene—God sitting on His throne while heavenly creatures of fire fly all around Him crying out, "Holy, holy, holy is the LORD Almighty. The whole earth is full of his glory."[4]

Face-to-face with a holy God, Isaiah is overcome with a tremendous sense of his own inadequacy and unworthiness. He cries out, "Oh, no! I'll be destroyed. My lips are filthy, I'm not pure, and I live among people who aren't pure."[5]

Isaiah's response is perfectly understandable. He doesn't plead for mercy, probably because he felt like his case was hopeless. I can certainly understand why he felt this way. It's all too easy to feel like we don't measure up when we compare ourselves to those around us—how much more so when standing in front of God! It may be because of our sins, our mistakes, or the circumstances of our past. However, the reality is, before God we are *all* in the same boat. Before Him all comparisons are meaningless.

But watch what happens to Isaiah next: God sends an angel to pick up a live burning coal that was so hot the Bible says the angel had to use tongs just to pick it up! The angel brings the coal over to Isaiah and places it on his lips, declaring: "Look, your guilt is taken away, because this hot coal has touched your lips. Your sin is taken away."[6]

Did you catch that? The very first thing the angel says to Isaiah isn't, "Your sins are forgiven." No, right off the bat he says, *"Look! Your guilt is all gone!"* Why do you suppose the angel addresses Isaiah's guilt first before he addresses his sin? I don't think the order of his words are a coincidence; I personally believe there's a deeply meaningful reason for this.

God knows our struggle with guilt is a powerful tool the devil wields to wreak destruction in our lives. We often acknowledge with our minds and our words that God has forgiven us, but all the while we remain stuck in our guilt and seldom experience—deep down in our souls—the joy and freedom of living each day totally guilt free and forgiven.

Standing in the presence of a holy, perfect God, Isaiah feels overwhelmed by guilt over his sins, and he justifiably expects to receive the full punishment for what he had done. By placing the fiery coal on Isaiah's lips and speaking words of mercy and grace, God is addressing Isaiah's feelings of responsibility for his sins and letting him know there's no need to feel guilt anymore because he's been completely cleansed of his sins.

Throughout the Bible fire is depicted as a symbol of God's holiness, presence, judgment, power, illumination, and purification.[7] The angel touches Isaiah's lips with the burning coal, because that's where he's most conscious of his guilt. (Remember, he cried out, "My lips are filthy.")

So what does this whole story about God, Isaiah, and the angel mean for you? One simple truth: *God does not want you to* feel *guilty, because in His eyes, you* aren't *guilty.* Are there consequences to sin? Absolutely. But God's Word says:

> If we own up to our sins, God shows that He
> is faithful and just by forgiving us of our sins
> and purifying us from the pollution of all the
> bad things we have done.[8]

If you've truly repented and asked God for His forgiveness, then great news! You've been forgiven and your guilt is gone! If you're still feeling guilty over a situation or a perceived failure on your part to not live up to your expectations or those of someone else, then expose that lie and replace it with the truth!

Whatever season God has you in, wherever He has placed you, don't allow your guilt to destroy what He wants to do *in you* and *through you.*

Let go of the guilt. Only you can free yourself of this

feeling. When the devil tries to make you feel guilty, remind yourself (and him) about the truth of what God says—your guilt is *gone!* Vanished! Defunct! Deceased! No more!

All those days, weeks, months, and maybe even years spent feeling guilty about what you've done or haven't done is over. In God's mind you aren't just "not guilty"—you are 100 percent "innocent and free"!

Now, *that's* worth getting excited about, isn't it?

Chapter Seven

CHOSEN

Adana Wilson

Surrender isn't the act of cleaning yourself up
until you're good enough for Christ. It's admitting
you never will be and accepting grace anyway.[1]
JON ACUFF

*I*N THE LAST chapter we talked about flipping the
script of your story and living guilt free. It takes both
letting go of the guilt and *receiving* grace.

You may have gotten to the point where you can
say, "Yeah, I know God's wiped away my guilt and He's
forgiven me." But that doesn't necessarily mean you're
living every single day out of the power and freedom
that come from *receiving* God's grace.

I'm heartbroken whenever I meet a woman who,
over the course of a conversation, tells me she knows
God has forgiven her, but she still wrestles with feeling

guilty on a *daily* basis...whatever the reasons may be. If that's you, I would love to sit down with you over a glass of Diet Dr. Pepper and share something with you. But since that can't happen, I want you to take a minute, forget what's going on around you, take a deep breath, and listen. I mean *really* listen carefully to what I'm about to say to you (and imagine I have a really sweet calm and soothing voice). Got it? OK, now let these words wash over your soul:

> I understand! I know what it's like to mess up for the hundredth time. I know what it's like to feel like you have to be perfect and to lose hope and feel like you're never going to get it right. To know in your head that God loves you, but still feel like you are not good enough. I've been there. But do you realize it doesn't have to be this way? You don't have to ever wake up with that awful, overwhelming feeling of guilt ever again. You never have to feel shame weighing you down and suffocating you till you can barely breathe. I know it sounds too good to be true. But believe me, it's not! You know about God's grace. You've read about it, heard sermons about it, even sang about it. The thing is, you've never *received* it. Or, if you have, you've forgotten to receive it again and again and again. Grace is a gift God

is offering you every second of every day. All
you have to do is be willing to *receive* it.

How often do you ask God to forgive you for something you've done but you don't ever forgive yourself?
As women, most of us are atrocious receivers. We've
fallen for a bill of lies from the time we were young
girls that we have to *earn* our rewards and nothing is
ever free. We've believed that we're the "inferior" sex,
and we have to sweat and slave over every word of the
story we're trying to write with our lives. But nothing
could be further from the truth.

Imagine you're a mother (unless, of course you are,
in which case you obviously don't have to imagine).
Christmas is right around the corner. You've been planning and picking out gifts for your kids. Some of us are
slight overachievers and started searching for the perfect gifts back in July, while others of us are finishing
up our shopping as the stores are closing on Christmas
Eve (I would fall into that category). No matter our
shopping process, our hearts are the same. We want to
pick out the perfect gift (and, we hope, at a really great
price) for our kids.

Christmas morning rolls around, and you're on pins
and needles with anticipation, because you cannot *wait*
to see their reactions. You just *know* they're going to
love the gifts you spent so much time and effort picking
out for them. Finally it's time, and your kids tear into
their gifts. You ask your daughter, "So, what do you

think?" She gets up from the floor where she's been sitting and gives you a hug, "Yeah, this is really cool, Mom. Thanks so much for getting this for me, but you know I just can't receive this gift from you." Speechless and flabbergasted for a few moments, you manage to eke out a question, "Umm…what? Why not?" Matter-of-factly your daughter responds, "Oh, I can't receive such an extravagant gift, because I don't deserve it or do anything to earn it."

Isn't that what we do? We won't receive from God because we don't feel like we deserve it. *We think and act like we're God's employees instead of living as God's daughters.* This the opposite of what the Bible tells us:

> Even before he made the world, God loved us and chose us in Christ to be holy and without fault in his eyes. God decided in advance *to adopt us into his own family* by bringing us to himself through Jesus Christ. This is what he wanted to do, and it gave him great pleasure.[2]

> But when the right time came, God sent his Son, born of a woman, subject to the law. God sent him to buy freedom for us who were slaves to the law, *so that he could adopt us as his very own children.* And because we are his children, God has sent the Spirit of his Son into our hearts, prompting us to call out, "Abba, Father." Now you are no longer a slave but

God's own child. And since you are his child, God has made you *his heir.*[3]

For all who are led by the Spirit of God are *children of God.* So you have not received a spirit that makes you fearful slaves. Instead, you received God's Spirit *when he adopted you as his own children.* Now we call him, "Abba, Father." For his Spirit joins with our spirit to affirm that *we are God's children.* And since we are his children, *we are his heirs.* In fact, together with Christ we are heirs of God's glory.[4]

One of the coolest aspects of adoption to me is how a child who's been adopted by loving parents will always know that he or she was specifically *chosen.* There's nothing accidental about them being picked. It's not like the adoptive parents spent months waiting for their child and then all of a sudden drew a name out of a hat. Of course not! It was deliberate and intentional. If you're that child, you can forever rest secure in the knowledge that you were adopted because your parents chose *you*…and only you.

That's you and me too! We were hopeless and lost until God rescued us, adopted us, and made us His daughters. And not just a daughter who lives under His roof and eats some of His food. No, you are God's *heir*! How incredible is that! You get to share in God's inheritance—not because of anything you've done or haven't done but simply because you are His daughter.

God has already written out the story of your life, and get this—it's the most incredible, beautiful, epic story ever written. But you have a choice. You can either choose to live out each day of the script He's written for you—*a script where you're brave and free and full of life.* Or you can go off script and choose to live out your own life—having to wrestle with your guilt by yourself, doing your own thing, and having to make all of your decisions based on your own limited knowledge— a knowledge that ultimately leads to death.

Which choice sounds better to you?

If you're dealing with guilt because of something you've done wrong or because you feel like you're not doing enough, I want to give you some practical keys for how you can live bravely and free from the suffocating burden of guilt.

First, break the power of your guilty feelings by confessing them to God. And then receive His forgiveness and His grace. For a lot of us, that is an act of our will. We choose to receive His forgiveness and grace rather than our own thoughts or feelings.

Next, you have to forgive yourself. Whether your guilt stems from a wrong you've committed or from not living up to your own expectations or someone else's, you have to forgive yourself and let go of the guilt. You have to tell the voice in your mind that God has not called or created you to be perfect. Forgive yourself and free yourself from that wrong expectation.

If you're struggling with feeling like you're not measuring up or doing enough, ask God to reveal what His priorities are for your life. Find out what He requires of you, and then evaluate if your priorities are in line with His. I promise this will make it much easier to say no without feeling guilty.

As a feeling, guilt is nothing more than an emotion. That's all it is. And when you take the time and effort to care for yourself, you're far less likely to be held captive by your emotions. Trim down your schedule. (I know how hard that is. Remember, I'm a working mom of three boys. But the effort is so worth it.) Spend time talking with God and hearing Him respond to you. Make it a priority to get enough rest. And be sure to have some fun in your life—do whatever it is that refreshes you, rejuvenates you, and gives you life. *When you take care of yourself, it's much easier to combat any guilty feelings.*

Finally, choose to walk in truth. The bottom line is, if you've confessed to God your guilt and any actions that may have caused that guilt, then God has *already* forgiven you. That's it. Any feeling of guilt you have that contradicts this is utterly false. And just to reinforce this point, I want to share some encouraging words from the author of Hebrews:

> Let us go right into the presence of God with sincere hearts fully trusting him. For *our guilty consciences have been sprinkled with Christ's blood to make us clean*, and our bodies have been washed with pure water.[5]

As I said earlier, your guilty feelings are based on your emotions—not on truth. Remind your soul—your mind, will, and emotions—what the truth is: you are God's daughter, and *because He's forgiven you, your guilt is gone.* And then every morning when you wake up, choose to receive God's grace and walk in that truth throughout the entire day. I love how Max Lucado puts it: "When grace moves in...guilt moves out."[6]

God doesn't want you to live your life burdened by guilt. Jesus bore your guilt, shame, and sin *so you don't have to.* Jesus died so you could have life—and not just a humdrum, boring, pointless life. He did it so you could have a life better than you could have ever dreamed.[7] Your job is to receive His gift of grace and forgiveness and start living with more joy, courage, and freedom than you've ever had before!

You've been chosen. Now it's your turn to start living like it.

Section 3

THE POWER OF
OUR CHOICES

*I'd like you to meet
my friend Lynda...*

EVERY SECOND OF every day we're bombarded with choices—whether to act or do nothing, to give a loving response or one that wounds, to extend our faith or retreat in fear. No matter where you live or what you do during "normal business hours," you know as well as I do that not all choices are created equal. For example, if I'm dieting (or trying to) after the holidays, my desire for chocolate is exponentially stronger. And so it requires me to exercise more strength of will in order to make a choice that aligns with my goals. Humans in general, and perhaps Americans specifically, tend to view choices through the filter of: Is it comfortable or is it good for us?

My dear friend Lynda Grove, who has faithfully

served in ministry with me for many years, knows all about choices. In this next chapter she skillfully walks us through the power of our daily choices—for good or for evil. Whether we realize it or not, each time we make a decision, we end up aligning ourselves with *something*. Lynda helps us see the best way to align so we can experience a healthy, fruitful life.

I've been friends with Lynda for decades—that's right, *decades*. And in all that time I have never seen her represent the Lord in a less than pleasing manner. Lynda and her husband, Kevin, are the caliber of friends everyone wants. They have traveled with Robert and me all around the world, and we could write a whole other book on those adventures and the food we refused to eat. Speaking of food, we do not have a shared passion for cooking—that is *all* her! I'm so excited for you to learn from the wealth of her wisdom as you begin to view your choices like stakes in the ground that mark out your territory or act as boundary lines. In the end, Lynda recognizes our dependence on God and gives us some amazing daily declarations to help set the tone for our entire day.

Chapter Eight

DISCOVERING YOUR RHYTHM

It's choice—not chance—that
determines your destiny.[1]
JEAN NIDETCH

*H*AVE YOU EVER awakened from a sweet night of rejuvenating, blissful sleep only to find that your feet have landed on the wrong side of the bed? You open your eyes, your feet barely brush against the carpet, and it begins. *Nothing* seems to fall into place. What usually takes only a moment to accomplish explodes into a rippling multitude of turmoil and bad attitudes.

You find yourself scolding the dryer for making your skinny jeans *extra* skinny, you trip over the dog, you're running late, and you're hopelessly searching for your missing keys. And it always seems like those are the days when you're bombarded with a defeating onslaught of unwelcomed events. Those are the days when the script of your story feels like a Top 10 list for "You Know It's a Bad Day When…"

As you leaf through David's personal journals in the Book of Psalms, you see he can *totally* relate to those "waking up on the wrong side of the bed" kind of days. In chapter after chapter he expresses the inner turmoil of his frustrations, his fears, and his failures as he walks through discouraging days and seasons in his life.

Time and time again he acknowledges the reality of his circumstances only to stop and redirect his course. What changes is not his circumstances but how he looks at them. He's saying, "This is what I'm dealing with today, but I don't have to stay here." We see him disciplining himself, *choosing* to seek, believe, wait, hope, trust, forgive, stand, and praise.

David has discovered a rhythm—a hidden secret—to walking through these challenging moments with confidence. He doesn't give in to despair. He chooses to declare that God is his strong fortress. Even when he's in the midst of a battle, David professes his victory long before his triumph comes.

Like the rhythm of his psalms, the rhythm of continuously choosing to believe God will come through for him becomes the sureness to his steps. He's not just choosing to look at it positively, but rather choosing to courageously trust that God can and *will* take his circumstances and flip them rightside up.

I've had many an "upside down" day full of toddlers and diapers, timeouts and tears, spilled milk and burnt dinners. The possibility of discouragement and defeat can loom over my spirit ready to seize control of my day. However, in a moment of choice, God can speak:

> As for me, I look to the LORD for help. I wait confidently for God to save me, and my God will certainly hear me. Do not gloat over me, my enemies! For though I fall, I will rise again. Though I sit in darkness, the LORD will be my light.[2]

Like David, I can *choose* to believe God's faithfulness and declare my confidence in Him. The choices I make and how I look at my day determine which way my day goes. I can set my anchor in the bedrock of God's faithfulness, and that choice will steer me through any circumstance I find myself in.

Whatever you choose will ultimately lead and guide you. As it was with David, your choices set your course and determine your path.

You can choose to listen to all the voices surrounding you and let them dictate your script. Or you can choose to let your script be penned day by day and choice by choice by God as you completely surrender control of your story to Him.

It's all too easy to be driven by whims and emotions, but when you begin to truly understand and tap into the power of your choices, you'll be able to consistently rise above any unbelief, doubt, or fear that comes your way. Instead of being unsure about God's perfect love and complete protection, you'll draw strength from your firm confidence in God's faithfulness.

Contrary to what so many believe, it's not your thoughts that establish your belief system; it's your choices. If, for example, you *think* that the church as a whole should be doing more to help people who don't have much or who can't stand up for themselves, but you yourself don't choose to do anything about it, then it's not really a core belief of yours. On the other hand, if you say you believe followers of Jesus are called to help the helpless and you're actually *making choices to live that out*, then yes, it's obviously a core component of your belief system.

I came face-to-face with determining what I truly believe a few years ago when I was a stay-at-home mom with four teenagers. My husband traveled quite a bit, so it was a lonely season in my life. Isolation led to insecurity in many areas, including my trust in God's plan for my family.

It was one of the most difficult times I've ever had to face. My heart truly wanted to trust the Lord, but somehow my faith kept falling miserably short. And then, just when I thought God was going to break through in my circumstances, everything curved in a direction I never expected. I was crushed. *All* hope seemed to be gone.

I remember standing there feeling emotionally paralyzed. No words. I felt utterly abandoned by God and was completely void of emotion. I couldn't even cry.

Suddenly my heart began to speak that the purpose for my family wasn't dependent on my circumstances. I knew *His* plan for our family was bigger than what I could see, and that even if I didn't understand every curve along the way, I had a choice to make. I could choose to trust Him and wait for His timing, or I could just keep falling and failing on my own. If my true desire for my family was to be in the center of *His* will, I needed to choose to look to Him as my source of strength, peace, and joy.

I stood there, set my feet firmly in place, and declared out loud: "I *will* stand."

I'll never forget that moment. In an instant I *knew* everything had changed. I knew God was moving on my behalf.

A few months later that curve became the biggest blessing in my life. It led me to new friends, greater opportunities for my children, and a long-awaited career change for my husband.

Every day you and I face choices. Some are subtle; some are complex; some are complicated by emotions and confused by obscurity. There are days when it's simple. You wake up and immediately sense God's presence and enjoy His goodness. Or you're easily able to look up from whatever chaos you're in and decide, "Since today's a day that God created and decided He wanted me to see, I'm going to find joy in it!"[3] Other days it takes every ounce of your courage to declare, "I *will* trust You."

Regardless of what kind of day you're having or what you're feeling, choose to put your confidence and trust in God and declare His faithfulness. You too will see His goodness!

Here are some declarations to God I like to use when I wake up to find my feet on the wrong side of the bed. I hope they will help you find your rhythm.

- Today...I'm going to wait on You and listen for Your voice.

- Today...I'm going to praise You regardless of my circumstances.

- Today...I'm going to be courageous, knowing You're with me and will never leave or forsake me.

- Today...I'm going to rest in the promises of Your Word.

- Today...I'm going to walk with confidence because I know You're in control of my life.

- Today...I'm choosing *You*.

It is incredibly freeing when you make the choice to trust that God is in control of every single day—that He's writing the script *He* wants. Whether it's now or later, He *always* comes through!

Section 4

DISCOVERING "I AM"

*I'd like you to meet
my friend Jan . . .*

EVERYONE DREADS GETTING a late-night phone call from a friend or family member with bad news. It's infinitely more difficult when the bad news is about you. Strong and courageous doesn't begin to describe the way I see my sweet friend Jan Greenwood. Our entire church and staff were inspired watching her walk so gracefully through an unexpectedly shocking cancer diagnosis. During that season we had many honest conversations and prayers about her fears and the confusion from trying to understand the unimaginable.

But Jan had an encounter with God that changed everything, and in the next few chapters she details that amazing moment when God declared His name to her. This was so much more than an FYI or reminder of what she already knew; He was answering *much more* than her sincere questions about healing. "I AM" is a declaration of God's character, a promise for the future, and tender comfort for the present. Jan shows us how once you know who God is, you learn who you are and are then prepared to make the choices necessary to plug into His Spirit, making Him your only Source.

Next, Jan breaks down the components of our souls while brilliantly illustrating the importance of aligning our will with God's will in order to really live the abundant life God planned for us. Finally she reminds us of the immense power found in our faith, even when it's as tiny as a single mustard seed. I love Jan dearly. She is so full of life and laughter; she is a hero to many and truly a woman of many talents and roles, including her most prized role as a wife and mom.

Chapter Nine

AN ANCHOR YOU
CAN CLING TO

Jan Greenwood

If the life of a man or woman on earth is to
bear the fragrance of heaven, the winds of
God must blow on that life, winds not always
balmy from the south, but fierce winds from
the north that chill the very marrow.[1]
ELISABETH ELLIOT

WHETHER WE LIKE it or not, adversity is a part of
life. If you live long enough, you're guaranteed to run
into some hurdles. It might be a physical hurdle or a
relational hurdle. Or it may be a financial, spiritual,
or mental one. The question isn't whether you'll face
adversity; rather, it's what are you going to do when
adversity comes.

I've certainly had my own portion of adversity in my

life. I want to share with you a little bit of my personal story so that you can be prepared when adversity enters your life. More importantly, I want to share about how you can walk through powerfully and emerge victorious on the other end. If you'll stick with the truths I'm about to share and implement them in your life, I honestly believe they will, at the very least, help you navigate through adversity with faith and hope, and, at best, they may just save your life.

It's in adversity that some of the best chapters of our stories are written. As we walk through challenging circumstances, we face some of the most important choices of our lives. We have a unique opportunity to cooperate with God to redirect, reorient, and even rewrite our outcomes. So let's dive into part of my story of adversity.

I've never been very good at taking care of myself. Taking care of everyone else in my family—my husband, daughter, and three sons? No problem. But myself? Not so much.

In June of 2009 that caught up with me. I'd just been through an eighteen-month period that had been one of the most stressful seasons of my life. Our family had relocated to a new city. I had just put my kids in public school after years of homeschooling. My husband, Mark, was on a job assignment out of state for a year. We moved my mom to our new community, and I bought a house and moved our family all within this period of time. I didn't have time or a need to find a new family doctor. Despite the fact that a few years earlier I had a suspicious mammogram, I wasn't prioritizing a screening. In fact, during those eighteen months, I scheduled my mammogram three separate times, and *all three times* I canceled my appointment because I was just too busy.

One day I sat down in the chair in my office, and I felt a searing pain shoot through my hip. It was so sharp I could hardly get up from the table. For the next couple of weeks every time I'd get up or down, it would hurt. I thought I had developed some kind of soft tissue injury—maybe a pulled muscle or damaged tendon; it would start to get better, and then suddenly it would be awful again. I did my usual self-diagnosis and believed it would just go away. This went on for months, and it got to the point where I couldn't wear high heels at all, and I was starting to drag my leg a bit.

All the while I was working hard, taking care of my family, and planning to go on a mission trip to Egypt with a group of women from my church. One evening, as I limped into the kitchen, my husband saw how I was hurting and kindly gave me an ultimatum: "If you don't go and get that taken care of, you're not going to be able to go to Egypt." That was enough to kick me in gear. The next day I scheduled an appointment to see a doctor, because I was determined that *nothing* was going to stop me from going to Egypt.

So in the early summer of 2009 I finally took the first step to take care of myself. I scheduled an appointment with an orthopedist and two days later went in for an MRI of my hip.

A week later the MRI results came in. The doctor opened his computer and showed my husband and me the MRI scan. When he got to the portion of my hip where I'd been experiencing pain, he explained that the tissue was soft and expanding, and that could potentially be indicative of a tumor. Stunned by the implications of his words, we just stared at him. Mark and I remained calm when he said he wanted to run some additional tests.

The following Monday I went to the hospital for a bone scan. While I was having the bone scan, the nurse casually asked me, "So, have they found your source tumor?" I lay there stunned and shocked as tears began to roll down my cheeks. *Wait a second…so not only do I have cancer, but it's in two places?* The nurse continued matter-of-factly, "It's hardly ever bone cancer. It's almost always metastasized. When was the last time you had a mammogram?"

I moved down the hall to breast radiology, where they immediately conducted a mammogram. They took me to another room and did an ultrasound. A few minutes later the radiologist came in and bluntly told me, "You have breast cancer, and it's metastasized to your hip. We need to get you to an oncologist ASAP."

That's how I discovered I had Stage IV breast cancer. The tumor in my breast was tiny; that's why I hadn't detected it at all. Well, that and the fact that I hadn't been paying any attention to my own health. The cancer was aggressive and growing quickly. Within a week, I had an MRI, a bone marrow biopsy, a biopsy of my hip, a needle biopsy in my breast, a PET scan, and a medical port put in. There was a lot of adversity in a short period of time.

A few weeks after I began chemotherapy, my husband and I went to a special Sunday night service at our church. I looked around and saw everyone worshipping, but I felt so exhausted and weary, I just didn't have the emotional or physical strength to engage. So I sat down in my seat and closed my eyes.

That's when I had an encounter with God like nothing I'd ever experienced before. When I closed my eyes, I felt like I entered a room where Jesus was waiting for me. I remember seeing Him and having a very direct one-on-one conversation with Him. To be honest, I actually was disrespectful and confrontational. I unloaded all of my doubts, my fears, my questions, and my pain, and I asked point-blank if He was punishing me. The entire time I was venting, Jesus didn't respond. He just let me unpack everything I was feeling and thinking until I ran out of steam. Finally I stopped and asked Him the question that was truly on my heart, "Are You going to heal me?"

And Jesus responded: *I Am.*

OK, let's pause the story here for a moment and let me try to explain the full weight and significance of that response. In the Bible there is another unusual encounter when God met Moses at a burning bush to call him to go back to Egypt and deliver the Israelites from the oppressive rule of Pharaoh. Moses wasn't feeling too sure about what he was hearing:

> But Moses protested to God, "Who am I to appear before Pharaoh? Who am I to lead the people of Israel out of Egypt?" God answered, "I will be with you. And this is your sign that I am the one who has sent you: When you have brought the people out of Egypt, you will worship God at this very mountain." But Moses protested, "If I go to the people of Israel and tell them, 'The God of your ancestors has sent me to you,' they will ask me, 'What is his name?' Then what should I tell them?" God replied to Moses, "I AM WHO I AM. Say this to the people of Israel: I AM has sent me to you."[2]

Moses asked God His name, and He responded "I AM WHO I AM." What does that even mean? To us, it may seem pretty cryptic at first glance. But to Moses, *God's name revealed His character.* It meant that nothing and no one can even begin to define God except God Himself. It meant that *what He says and what He does are all wrapped up in who He is.*

Does that help to shed some light on why Jesus responded to me the way He did?

I believe God was saying the same thing to me that

He was saying to Moses: "Jan, I am enough for you. I am aware. I will bring it to pass. I will go with you."

When I heard Jesus say, "I Am," there was a wealth of meaning in those two tiny words. He was both reminding me of who He was *and* answering my question. He wasn't saying it was going to be easy; I knew I was going to face some massive battles. I wasn't even sure He was literally going to heal me. But I knew He had spoken to me and was going to be right there with me. *Jesus's reminder about who He is gave me an anchor to cling to.* I knew He was saying, "*No matter what, I Am sufficient.*" And that, in itself, was more than enough for me.

From that moment on—whatever the context— whenever I've heard someone say the words, "I am..." or I've said them myself, I always remember what Jesus said to me, and I draw strength from it.

And so I chose to believe He was going to heal me—and He did. I walked through a long and grueling season of treatment, surgery, and recovery. I lost my hair, part of my breast, and a lot of my pride. I didn't get to make that trip to Egypt. But nonetheless, I found Him faithful. Every day He proved that He is who He is. I am so grateful to tell you that I have been completely cancer-free for several years! My healing is a reminder to me that He is enough for all of us— cancer-free or not, He is enough.

When you come up against some adversity or storm in your own life, and you feel like there's no possible way for you to overcome such a massive obstacle, I want you to remember God's name—I Am.

Even though you can't handle it, *He* can. It's simple. But it's profound.

I Am is in control and ever present. And regardless of the raging storm you're facing, that's an anchor you can always cling to.

Chapter Ten

YOU CHOOSE

Jan Greenwood

> Destiny is not a matter of chance; it is a
> matter of choice. It is not a thing to be
> waited for; it is a thing to be achieved.[1]
> WILLIAM JENNINGS BRYAN

ONCE YOU HAVE a revelation of God's faithfulness and His great love for you, you will be able to make wise choices in the midst of unexpected storms. Whatever you've been through or whatever you may yet face, God is faithful. His power, presence, and love will carry you through.

In the last chapter I shared about my struggle with cancer and what God spoke to me in the middle of that situation to remind me of these truths. Now I want to give you a practical key God shared with me so that you and I can stand strong and not get swept away by unexpected storms.

The Bible tells us about Job, who, in the span of *minutes*, experienced some of the greatest adversity and most devastating losses imaginable. When Job woke up that morning, it seemed all was right with his world. But by nightfall devastation was everywhere. First, he suffered a massive business and economic loss when his stock of farm animals, sheep, and even his camels and all those who cared for them were stolen and struck down in one harsh blow. While still reeling from this news, a message arrived that was beyond belief. In one fell swoop all of his sons and daughters had been killed by a natural disaster.

This was more than Job could handle on his own. The Bible tells us that he stood and tore his robe in grief, then shaved his head and fell to the ground to call out to God.[2]

Can you imagine how Job must have felt being assaulted with such tragic news? And then get this. You'd think it couldn't *possibly* get any worse for Job, right? But it did.

Job lost his health, his employees and finances, his children, and heaping insult upon injury, his wife mocked him for his faith—and yet he refused to deny God.[3]

How on earth do you go through a series of devastating tragedies like that and still trust God? How do you keep going when you feel like giving up because life seems like a never-ending uphill battle? In those tough seasons the Bible urges us to stay the course:

> Let's keep a firm grip on the promises that keep us going. *He always keeps his word.*[4]

I know some of you who are going through a challenging and confusing season might be thinking, "Yeah, that's easy enough to say when things are going well, but it sure doesn't feel that way to me now." I understand. I know exactly what's it like to *think* and *feel* like God's not keeping up His end of His agreement.

But it doesn't have to stay that way. This is the moment when you can begin to rewrite your story. If tragedy has struck or grief is present, you have the choice and the opportunity to flip the script. It isn't that I'm in denial of the realities you may be facing, but rather I know the power and peace available to you when you simply choose to align your will with the heart of God. Let me explain what I mean.

Every single person—whether man or woman—is made up of three core parts: body, soul, and spirit:

> May God himself, the God who makes everything holy and whole, *make you holy and whole, put you together—spirit, soul, and body—*and keep you fit for the coming of our Master, Jesus Christ.[5]

Body. Soul. Spirit. Three parts. One person. Does that remind you of anything? God is three—Father, Son, Holy Spirit—and yet also one.

Our body is the physical part of us—our appearance, our physical health, our strength, and our senses (sight, sound, touch, taste, and hearing).

Our soul also has three parts consisting of our mind (thoughts, reasoning, logic, common sense, and knowledge), our emotions (feelings, temperament, and concerns), and our will (wishes, desires, and choices).

Our spirit is our direct link to God connecting us to a supernatural source of power, wisdom, and strength.

When you view these three distinct parts from this perspective, you can see our soul—our mind, emotions, and will—functions like a bridge between the supernatural and the natural. It connects our spirit with our body. It allows us to be "in this world" but not "of this world." (If this all feels a little philosophical and abstract to you, please bear with me just a little longer. I *promise* we're going somewhere with all of this.)

Let me give you a picture to consider. Could you imagine for me that your soul is like a power strip? You know, the kind that has one end that you plug into your wall outlet and on the other end has a multi-plug adapter to distribute the power to multiple sources. You can *try* to plug that power strip into all kinds of things, but unless it's plugged into a working outlet—an active power source—it's never going to work the way it was created to.

We are just like that. All of us have a need for power. We have an innate desire to draw strength from something or someone. Yet we are fashioned to be connected to one power source and one alone—God. It's only when we "plug in" to God through our belief in Jesus Christ that we experience real power. We can't create or access power by ourselves. Thank goodness, we don't have to. When you plug your power strip (or soul) into the right power source (God), you're connecting to a long-term, fully sustainable, untainted power source.

When we don't draw our strength from God, we try and plug our souls into all kinds of other things—a career, status, money, spouse, kids, boyfriend or girlfriend, alcohol, TV, pornography, social media, shopping, food, sports, working out—basically anything that will give us the quick sense of control we need to get through the day. But plugging into any of these power sources is only a temporary fix and is as unnatural to our souls as plugging a power strip into a flower pot. It just won't work the way it's supposed to. People whose souls *aren't* plugged into God are in effect trying to write the script of their story on their own. They have an ever-present, unfilled craving for power.

Let's imagine that power strip again. On the opposite end of the wall plug lies the multi-plug adapter. This is the real workhorse of the power strip—the bridge between the source of power and the release of power. Imagine with me for a moment that you have a three-prong adapter. One prong represents your mind, one represents your emotions, and one represents your will. Even though there are three choices, you can plug your computer, lamp, or appliance into only one adapter. How will you choose?

Some people tend to "plug in" through their mind and are often driven by a need to know. Just think about it (pun intended). How many times have you struggled endlessly to understand the why or how of something? How many times have you said to God, "I just don't understand"? I can easily become so obsessed with knowing that my mind runs rampant, and I lose sleep, totally forgetting the mystery of God and the importance of faith and trust. In addition, when I am focused on what I know over who God is, I can become an information junkie and a know-it-all. This kind of power connection leads to an unsatisfied craving for knowledge (it's never enough) and a lack of peace. It's not that we shouldn't seek understanding, but that we can't demand understanding over trust in God.

Some people "plug in" through their emotions—what they *feel*. All girls know that depending on your emotions leaves you bouncing on a seesaw of confusion. *Everything* becomes about how you feel at the moment. If you *feel* good today, you are good. If you *feel* bad, you are bad. Sometimes you feel both at the same time, which naturally leads to confusion and double-mindedness. Using your power strip through the adapter of your emotions produces volatile and inconsistent fruit of the Spirit (power) in your life— one day it's sweet and juicy; the next it's sour and rancid.

But what happens if you "plug in" through the adapter of your will? What if you make a conscious decision to set your will in agreement with God? (This is such great news!) When you align your will with God's will, you access a power that brings your entire soul (mind, emotions, will) into order and alignment with God. You experience a power surge! Your spirit is now free to flow through your soul and impact your body. This is what happens when a person first experiences salvation or every time we encounter God in a moment of prayer or worship. There is an instant release of strength, peace, and power.

If I plug a power strip into an outlet on a wall and then plug a lamp into the multi-prong adapter and turn the switch on, what happens? The lamp lights up, right? But does the lamp light up out of its own power? Does it decide on its own when it wants to shine? Does it have any capacity of its own to move because it doesn't like the view from where it's standing? No, the lamp is fueled by the source of power that runs to it through the power strip.

That's how your body operates too. When your will "plugs in" to your spirit, it sets your mind on the right course of thinking life-giving thoughts. What you think about now determines how you feel. How you feel becomes the catalyst for action, spurring your body to do what you tell it to do. In effect, you flip the switch and power is released. You become empowered by God. Your spirit, soul, and body begin to flow as one, moving from heaven to earth, from supernatural to natural.

Your will—specifically your free will—is *incredibly* powerful. It's part of God's very image in you.

Think about it. The simple fact that God created us with a free will is phenomenal. That God—who is all-powerful, all-knowing, all-sovereign—would allow you and me (who obviously aren't) to make our own choices is nothing short of mind-blowing.

Your free will is the key to getting through those really tough days and difficult seasons. It's a vital part of flipping the script of your story. You have the choice to access the power of God to go on, to grow strong, to hope again. Exercising your free will by aligning with God's will leads you to an enduring strength, a rich stability, and a confident expectation of His goodness, even in the midst of uncertainty or pain.

We are really talking about your ability to choose. *You* choose. When you don't plug your soul into God through the filter of your will, you let yourself be governed by the most casual, fleeting whims all day long. You end up thoughtlessly plugged into detrimental sources and situations.

Take a step back and look at your overall life—your relationships, your home, your career. Now consider that all you see is the result of your *decisions*, your *choices*, the setting of your will.

Is there an area of your life where you feel like you're

experiencing death? I want you to make an intentional choice with your will to *choose life* in that area.

Maybe you're thinking, "How do I just 'choose life'? I've tried everything to fix that area in my life; nothing's worked. You don't know me or my story. And you're telling me I can just choose life?"

If you were standing right in front of me, my answer to you would be the same one I'm going to give you now—yes, yes, yes! This is how you go through the storms of life and still trust God. You choose life.

Just before he died, Moses gave one final charge to the people of Israel whom he had led for so many years:

> Today I have given you *the choice between life and death*, between blessings and curses. Now I call on heaven and earth to witness the choice you make. *Oh, that you would choose life*, so that you and your descendants might live! You can make this choice by loving the LORD your God, obeying him, and committing yourself firmly to him. This is the key to your life.[6]

God doesn't force His will on us. He gives us a choice. He lets us decide whether we're going to plug into Him or something else, whether we're going to follow Him or reject Him. It's a life-and-death decision—and more than anything, God wants you to surrender your will to Him and *choose life*.

If you've been going through some circumstances

and feeling like God isn't for you and is, in fact, against you, I want you to know *that is a lie*.

I urge you to take your circumstances and ask God how *He* sees you and your situation. Be still and listen for His response. And then choose life—choose to believe His words and cling to them. Let your confidence and faith in Him rule over your thoughts and your feelings.

That's the first step to overcoming adversity.

In the next chapter we're going to talk about the second step. Fair warning though: it may stretch some of us out of our comfort zones. But when we consider what the alternative is to choosing life, it is *so* worth it!

Ready?

Chapter Eleven

SMALL FAITH, A BIG MOUTH, AND A GOOD GOD

Jan Greenwood

Faith is different from proof; the one is
human, the other is a gift of God.[1]
BLAISE PASCAL

*W*HEN I WAS first diagnosed with cancer, there were several times when well-meaning people said, "I bet God's really teaching you something through this process." And while God was definitely teaching me, what I heard them saying to me was, "The only way God could get your attention was to give you a disease." I know that's not what they meant, but that's how it felt.

I've heard other people say, "Just have more faith, and you'll be healed." It's almost as if they view faith like a faucet. You turn on the faith faucet, and *bam!*— you're healed. Turn it off…and you're not.

But that's simply not the way faith really works. Jesus explained it like this:

> If you had even a faint spark of faith, even faith as tiny as a mustard seed, you could say to this mountain, "Move from here to there," and because of your faith, the mountain would move. If you had just a sliver of faith, you would find nothing impossible.[2]

Jesus is telling us here that it's not a matter of having *more* faith; you only need as much faith as the size of a mustard seed. Have you ever seen a mustard seed? Do you know how miniscule mustard seeds are? They're usually about one to two millimeters in diameter—that's so tiny, you can't even split one with a kitchen knife! And, according to Jesus, that's all the faith that's required from me to move the mountain I'm facing.

But there's one additional and crucial, but often overlooked, step—Jesus tells us we have to open our mouths and speak to the mountain.

I've come across so many women who have gallons and gallons of faith, but they won't open their mouths for themselves and speak to the mountains in their way. It's not enough to make the decision to choose life—we have to audibly declare it.

Many of us have learned to speak to God, but we've never learned to speak to our mountain. And often we spend all our time asking God to do something for us that we've been commanded to do for ourselves. Jesus didn't say that God would find nothing impossible. It's easy enough for us to believe that. We know God can do anything.

It's much harder for us to believe what Jesus actually said, "You would find nothing impossible."

God used this truth to change my perspective and, in turn, revolutionize the way I pray for myself, my family, and my circumstances. I suddenly realized cancer was a gigantic mountain in my life standing on the road between me and my destiny—and I had to get it out of the way.

But because it was so much bigger than anything I could tackle all by myself, the only choice I had was to speak to it with the tiny sliver of faith I had and command it to get out of the way.

I had to learn to speak to an entire mountain range of cancer. I would speak to myself, my body, and I even had to learn to speak to fear. My prayer life became an ongoing movement between God and me and this mountain. I would turn my attention to God, draw from His love, then turn my attention to the mountains of cancer and fear and tell them to leave me alone. Finally I would even encourage myself in the Lord by declaring that I refused to die.

I have to admit, the very first time I spoke to cancer and told it to get out of my way, I didn't believe myself at all. As soon as I made a quality decision to choose life and said the words "I will not die," I heard a voice in my head saying, "You might."

So I said it again: "I'm not going to die—I'm going to live!" Once again I heard that voice in my head: "Oh, OK…we'll see."

And I know it wasn't just the devil who was talking to me. It was also me, speaking doubt to myself. My words were lining up with my faith, but my will wasn't quite plugged in. I was struggling to believe for my future, but I kept being reminded about my past.

You see, just three years earlier I had lost a best friend to cancer. For five years I was by her side and watched her walk through a devastating battle with breast cancer. She was a faithful friend who loved Jesus. Countless people were praying and fasting for her to be healed of the sickness ravaging her body. I dared to hope that God would heal her, and I remember praying: "God, now would be the most awesome time for You to glorify Yourself. Come on, it would be so good for Your reputation…just think about how many people would know that You had healed her!"

During this time I heard some people imply that she just needed more faith to be healed (which is the same thing as saying she didn't have enough faith). And honestly, I was afraid that might be true. The things I'd heard about how more faith is needed to overcome kept recycling over and over in my mind. I couldn't decide if all the tragic and awful things happening to my friend's body came from the devil or from God.

After my friend's death I wrestled and wrestled with the question: "Is God really good?"

During all those months God never once defended Himself or tried to persuade me of His goodness. He allowed me to choose for myself.

One day I came to a startling realization: God wasn't going to explain Himself or justify Himself to me. I had to give up on trying to rely on my relentlessly demanding thoughts. I couldn't be controlled anymore by my crushed emotions. I had to make a choice of my own free will and decide to agree with God about His goodness: "Lord, I don't understand. This situation is bad, but by faith I'm declaring that You are good!"

In that moment I surrendered everything—all of my confusion and disappointment. When I made a choice to agree with God about who He says He is, it was like the Grand Canyon opened up before me in my mind. I saw myself standing on the edge of a precipice, and in the chasm below me was the death of my friend and all my questions and heartache and difficulties I couldn't comprehend. I sensed myself back up and take a running leap, soaring across that chasm. As I landed on the other side, I said, "You're good. All that stuff down there is bad, but You are good."

Once I settled this critical question, it was easy for me to set my will in agreement with God and to believe that God's script for my life and for my friend's life was good, and not just page after page of senseless randomness.

I had to die to my demands. I had to die to my questions. I still don't understand. I don't get it. But you know what? I could spend my whole life looking into that pit and demanding that God explain Himself to me. Or I can leap over and choose to believe that He is good.

There is power in laying your pain, your questions, your fear, and your doubts down at the feet of Jesus and just admitting, "I don't get it, but I choose to trust You." And then (circling back to what we talked about at the beginning of the chapter) begin to speak aloud to your mountain with whatever amount of faith you have and tell it to move.

All you really need is small faith and a big mouth.

So what are you asking God for? What mountain are you facing?

Everything you need to overcome any adversity has already been given to you. When you learn to cooperate with God by aligning yourself with His perspective, you'll discover the strength you need to trust Him. And when your faith combines with your words and actions, you'll begin to see the most beautiful miracles in your life!

If you have no idea what it feels like to have the power of God pouring in and through your life, get up right now and start delving into God's Word and discovering what He's promised to you. Then make a quality decision to agree with Him and start speaking those promises from God's Word aloud. You will experience a power surge of the most beautiful kind, one that will propel you through adversity to hope and peace.

You don't have to be in a crisis to plug your will into the power source of the Holy Spirit. You don't have to wait for an extreme difficulty to get in alignment with God. As a matter of fact, please don't wait. If you're waiting to plug your will into the Holy Spirit until you're facing crisis, then you're going to walk into it already plugged into something that can't give life. It's so much easier to walk into a crisis already connected to the right Source.

Section 5

NAVIGATING THROUGH CONFLICT

*I'd like you to meet
my friend Mallory . . .*

*N*o ONE LOVES conflict. Most of us hate to even have hard conversations and end up finding ways to avoid them. We would much rather have peace. Peace is used as a greeting, a political statement, a wish for departing friends, or a saying for those who have passed away. Peace and quiet are every mom or older sibling's *dream*, yet most of us shy away from what's required to cultivate that peace in the face of conflict.

Mallory Bassham is *not* one of those people. She isn't one to shrink away from conflict; as a matter of fact, she can just as easily skydive out of plane with grace (she *loves* skydiving) as she can jump into a tense or heated conversation. If she believes a resolution can be reached, she'll go the distance to achieve it and teach you how too. Mallory has been a part of our team and a good friend of mine for several years now. She left the corporate world where it was normal to kick butt and take names in order to join our church staff where the culture was *quite* different.

Mallory is such a valuable member of our team, and she has done an incredible job helping to teach our staff all about conflict resolution through healthy communication. In the next couple of chapters she'll outline for you some incredibly practical and effective steps to lay down your battle weapons and instead pick up God-honoring tools to successfully navigate through conflict. She'll then teach us how to secure peace by employing some tried and true methods, which begin with the end in mind, elevate relationships, preserve unity, and honor God.

Chapter Twelve

BEING COURAGEOUS
IN CONFLICT

Mallory Bassham

Nothing moves forward in a story except
through conflict. Put another way, conflict
is to storytelling what sound is to music.[1]
ROBERT McKEE

EVERY GREAT STORY—WHETHER told through film,
the pages of a book, the silver screen, the Internet, or
simply words spoken—has five core elements: characters, setting, theme, plot, and a conflict to resolve.
Remove any one of these elements, and suddenly the
story simply isn't that great or flat out doesn't work.

Think about it. If you were to watch a movie where
none of the characters had any conflict, how interesting
do you think it would be? What would *The Princess
Bride* be like if Wesley and Buttercup stayed on the

farm the entire movie going about their daily chores and adoringly gazing into each other's eyes...and that's all you had to watch for an hour and a half? Or how compelling would *Pride and Prejudice* be if Mr. Darcy and Elizabeth Bennet knew they liked each other the first time they met and immediately decided to marry? And what would *The Sound of Music* be like if there were no Nazis or Baroness Schraeder?

But those are stories told in movies. I know we live in real life, where conflict is nowhere near as enjoyable to experience. Think about your life, though. How would your story look different if you had never had any conflict from the time you were born up until now? Would you be the person you are now?

Max Lucado says, "Conflict is inevitable, but combat is optional."[2] And that's so true. As much as we try to avoid conflict in our personal relationships, the reality is, it will *always* be present. The more easily you accept it, the more equipped you'll be to handle it.

Contrary to how agonizing it can often feel, conflict and confrontation can actually be extremely constructive. They challenge us to grow, to mature and to die to our need to always be right—to always win—but only when we seek to resolve disagreements through healthy communication and a proper perspective. Just like in every great story, the key is not in *avoiding* conflict but in *resolving* it.

Unfortunately I believe the art of resolving conflict is a lost tool for people in our society today. If you want to live out your story confidently and courageously, you have to start flipping the script by learning how you can effectively manage conflict by having loving, timely, and productive confrontations with the people in your life.

Virtually everyone has had a disagreement with a friend, a boss, a coworker, or someone who works for them. Even worse are those with your parents, your kids, and spouse.

How many times did those disagreements end badly? Now think back to those times when they didn't—when they ended well—can you pinpoint *why* you were able to resolve the conflict?

Most people resort to grabbing one of three tools when faced with conflict: a broom, a flashlight, or a megaphone. Those of us who grab brooms nonchalantly look around the room, and, when no one is watching, we quickly lift the carpet and with a swift *swish* of our broom sweep it out of sight and pretend like it never existed. Those of us who switch on our flashlights shine a steady blinding light on the conflict until it's the only thing people around ever notice. And then there are those of us who pick up megaphones and shout so loudly about our conflict that everyone around us wants to retreat and hide because of all the noise and confusion we cause.

Which one of those three tools do you grab? And let me bluntly ask...how well has that turned out for you? Based on my experience, *none* of those go-to tools are adequate or even remotely capable to help you deal with disagreements effectively.

I can't give you a magic wand to wave at all your disagreements and make them vanish. What I *can* do is give you practical ground rules and tips for navigating through the potential minefields of conflict. My goal and sincere desire is that when you finish reading this next chapter, you'll walk away confident in your ability to resolve disagreements in every sphere of your life.

So, let's get to it, shall we?

Chapter Thirteen

THE ART OF PEACE

Mallory Bassham

> The difference between spiritual and
> unspiritual community is not whether
> conflict exists, but is rather in our attitude
> toward it and our approach to handling it.[1]
> LARRY CRABB

W E ALL HAVE to deal with conflicts from time to time. But we often try to avoid them pretending and putting on a good face...until we eventually blow up. After we've blown it, we get so preoccupied with dealing with our bad behavior that the real issue remains unresolved. This is a big deal, because once you get caught up in focusing on your bad behavior, you hinder your ability to effectively address the core issue.

The Bible talks about how wonderful it is to walk in unity and how that should always be our end goal: "See how good and pleasant it is when brothers and sisters live together in harmony!"[2] Although we know conflict is inevitable, there are practical ways to prepare without either over-spiritualizing or denying your feelings, so you can consistently walk away while preserving unity and resolving the situation.

Ideally the best way to deal with conflict is to establish clear expectations, create accountability, and be very open and candid. Sometimes you have to set the stage with a person; otherwise, you'll highjack them. If you really want resolution to a conflict, you often have to prepare the other person for your conversation. Tell them up front: "My goal for us after this conversation is to continue down our path, with our arms linked together."

And I want to tell you…This. Really. Works.

PREPARE YOUR HEART

But before you walk into a confrontation with someone, your very first ground rule is to *prepare your heart*.

How do you do this? First, you ask God to give you wisdom and help you see the situation from His perspective. And then be sensitive to however the Holy Spirit guides you during the course of your conversation.

In the Bible David asked God to prepare his heart by praying:

> Explore me, O God, and know the real me.
> Dig deeply and discover who I am. Put me

to the test and watch how I handle the strain. Examine me to see if there is an evil bone in me, and guide me down Your path forever.[3]

Every morning when we wake up, we should echo those words—and especially so before we're about to walk into a confrontation. One time, as I was heading into a confrontation with a woman who reported to me, I heard the Holy Spirit say to me: *Just listen.* I immediately shot back: "Of *course*, I'm going to listen! That's why I'm going to meet her!" But that wasn't what I had been planning to do at all. My original plan was to go in there, show her where *she* was wrong, and wait for her apology. But wisdom prevailed, and I ultimately chose to listen to the Holy Spirit's direction.

When I went into this meeting, I really did listen. And as I did, I began to understand her perspective and see where she was coming from. The issue that needed to be resolved wasn't one of stubbornness and rebellion; it was one of unclear expectations. She expected me to act one way (based on *her* understanding), and I was acting in a different way (based on *my* understanding).

I didn't interrupt her...not even once. (And I was pretty proud of myself for that, because that is *not* easy for me.) When she was finished, I said, "I think I know what the breakdown is between us. I had no idea that's what you expected of me. If I had known that's what you expected, I know I would have tried to do it. But I had no idea, and I'm *really* sorry. I'm sorry you felt that way, and I'm sorry I disappointed you. Are we going to be OK?" She graciously said yes, and we continued to work together, only now with a better understanding of each other's perspective.

When confronting someone, always identify your motive. Are you trying to prove your point? Do you have to be right? Are you trying to prove that you're clever?

It's so important to ask yourself: "*Why* am I going to confront this person?" And then make sure that respect and honor are present in the room when you confront.

You also have to be willing to be transparent during your conversation. If you're not authentic, I guarantee the other person will spot your fakeness a mile away. Have you ever tried to resolve a situation with someone who you *knew* was lying to your face? It doesn't lead to anything productive, right?

Another major key in preparing your heart is to *make sure you sincerely want the best for the situation*. That doesn't mean you want what's best for *you*. It means you want what's best for *everyone* involved. You have to walk into a confrontation *willing to accept that you're wrong*. When it comes to conflict, both the foolish and the wise start at the same point—zero. The difference in the end on whether it gets resolved is your attitude, not your aptitude.

PREPARE WHAT YOU'LL SAY

The second ground rule is, *prepare what you'll say*.

Most of the time conflict springs up suddenly. It's

like you're going about minding your own business, and out of the blue you're hit by a freight train. You don't have time to prepare for it.

When that happens, remember to *step back*. Don't let your emotion hijack you or the situation. It's easy to jump into defense or offense mode and try to do things like hold your ground, stand on principle, or prove you're right. But the best thing you can do is to step back—emotionally and sometimes even physically.

If you stay alert to the signals of escalation from the people in your life, you can often preemptively *step back, take an aerial look at the situation, and remain calm. You have to remove emotion from the equation.*

The key I want you to always remember is this: *you always have an option.*

If you're engaged in a conversation that's already too heated, take a time-out. Acknowledge that there's a heightened level of emotions and *ask for permission to regroup and revisit the discussion when you've both cooled down a bit.* Say: "You know, I don't think I'm communicating in a way that's super clear. Would it be possible for us to take a little break and regroup later? Because I really don't want to say anything I don't mean, and I feel like we're potentially heading down a hurtful path for both of us. I one hundred percent want to talk through this with you, but can we take a break from it for now?"

I've learned it's always going to better for me if I can remember to fall back on some reliable defusing

phrases when I'm in the middle of a conflict in order
to avoid letting emotions get the best of me. Here are
some I encourage you to use:

- Help me understand why it's difficult to
  tell me the truth.

- What else should I know?

- What would you like to see happen?
  (Remember, just because you want resolution doesn't mean the other person
  does.)

- I need to get something off my chest
  that I may have misunderstood.

- Let's work through this. We may or may
  not reach the answer, but I would like
  to try.

- Do you see the benefit in attempting to
  resolve this?

- I'm sorry. I didn't mean to hurt you.
  Please forgive me. You are so valuable to
  me, and I didn't show you that very well.

- How did you come to that conclusion?

- I want to work with you, but when you
  yell or use that kind of language, I find
  it difficult. Can we work through this
  together?

And if you *do* let your emotions hijack the situation and you feel like you've completely lost control of yourself, here's what you have to remember: you always have a choice. Every. Single. Time.

Daniel Goleman, author of *Emotional Intelligence: Why It Can Matter More Than IQ*, sums up why not allowing our emotions to hijack us can be beneficial:

> Emotional self-control—delaying gratification and stifling impulsiveness—underlies accomplishment of every sort.[4]

You want to accomplish something? *Don't let yourself be governed by your emotions.*

Years ago my youngest stepson kept talking about his hot temper and how he just couldn't help himself. So one day I sat down with him and explained that exhibiting a quick and fiery temper is a choice; it's not something inherent in our behavior.

Let me ask you: How did Jesus behave? Was He short-tempered all the time, screaming at everybody? No, except for one occasion (which was a demonstration of righteous anger at injustice), Jesus responded with patience, grace, kindness, and love...regardless of how exhausted He felt physically or emotionally.

As you prepare what to say, it's good to remember these three steps—*pause, ponder,* and *pray.* The Bible encourages us to:

> Trust GOD from the bottom of your heart; don't try to figure out everything on your own. Listen for GOD's voice in everything you do, everywhere you go; he's the one who will keep you on track. Don't assume that you know it all.[5]

> Plans fail for lack of counsel, but with many advisers they succeed.[6]

We need to trust God and listen for His voice, and also seek the advice of wise people in our lives. Whenever you receive (or give) advice, though, you should always check to make sure it lines up with the Word of God. And before you walk into a confrontation, ask God to help you be humble, gracious, wise, and submitted. Let Him show you how your words and emotions can line up with His Word. He promises to direct your steps and your words.

I've learned it's helpful for me to remember when I'm dealing with a relational conflict that all people are just sheep—you're a sheep; I'm a sheep. And even sheep who are saved because of God's unfathomable grace can sometimes be jealous, petty, egotistical, imperfect, irrational, demanding, and flat-out rude. Sometimes, ugly just comes out. And surprise, surprise...I'm guilty of it too!

I try not to be, but the truth of the matter is sometimes I am. And in those moments I have to humbly come before God—even though I'm embarrassed and ashamed—and tell Him I shouldn't have said those words or I should have held my temper. And I have to ask for forgiveness. And guess what? He is faithful to forgive me every time.

But having that awareness of my own occasional lapses into ugliness helps me to remember I'm relating to regular people, just like me.

On the flip side, even though we're all similar in that we're human, each of us is also uniquely different. (Have you ever taken a personality test? Those tests barely scratch the surface when it comes to how unique and different each of us is.)

People come from every type of background imaginable: unique childhoods and cultural influences; big families and small families; East Coast vs. West Coast; conservative, liberal, or independent. Even the oldest and youngest children in the same family will have a uniquely different view of the world.

And because of that, we each have our own set of baggage that we bring to a conflict. I don't have any idea about yours, and you don't know anything about mine. And that's why it's so vital for us to have *elasticity* in our attitudes toward others. (Side note: I just *love* elastic! Isn't it a marvelous invention? The older I get, the more I appreciate its presence in my clothes!)

Jesus encountered thousands and thousands of different individuals during His three years of ministry here on the earth. And time and time again we see Him consistently responding to each person with warmth, openness, and love. He always encouraged people to take their focus off of themselves and each other and to fix their focus on God. *That* is our model when it comes to confrontation and conflict.

The best way to follow Jesus's example is to draw close to Him and trust Him. You'll be amazed at what He'll do. Be confident in His leading and really be willing to listen—first to God and then to the person. Intentionally listening is crucial to resolution. Then, sincerely submit the situation to God with all of your heart and follow His direction and prompting.

PREPARE THE TIME AND PLACE

The final ground rule is, *prepare the time and place.*

Timing is everything, and approach is key. Esther took time to fast and pray before she went to see her husband, the king. So prepare your heart, and rid yourself of heated emotion. When would be a good time to bring it up? Purposefully choose a safe, nontoxic moment in your day so you avoid acting out of stress and escalating the situation.

Getting ready for church on Sunday mornings used to always be the most stressful time of the week for my family. We'd all run around the house frantically trying to get out the door suitably dressed and on time, and inevitably emotions would run high. Conversations like this were the norm:

"Where's my Bible? I can't find my Bible anywhere!"

"How should *I* know where your Bible is? I
have enough to keep track of. How come you
don't know where your Bible is? Have you not
had your devotions lately?"

Sunday mornings were definitely a toxic time for my
family. They were *not* an ideal time for me to say to
my husband, "Honey, I have something I want to talk
about with you."

I urge you to identify the toxic times in your
schedule. Ask yourself: "When do my emotions seem
to run higher than normal? When is it *not* going to be
super beneficial to bring up an issue (either for you or
for the person you're addressing)?"

Several years ago author Gary Smalley came to our
church and talked about something called the "Team
Win" concept. He said:

> Members of a team win together, or they lose
> together. Partners in a relationship experience
> exactly the same thing—except that in rela-
> tionships, you choose every day whether you
> will win or lose. What will you choose?[7]

That's so true, isn't it? When you and someone you're
in relationship with have a conflict, neither of you win
when a conflict ends with one person walking away as
"the winner."

My husband and I often go back to the "team win" concept when we have a conflict, and it does wonders for our perspective. For example, I *really* like for my kitchen to be clean. I like the sinks clean, the counters clean, the floors clean. And because I often cook, my husband handles kitchen cleanup duty.

This usually works out great for us, but during one period of time I started to get irritated because the kitchen wasn't looking as clean as I wanted it to. The dishrag in the sink looked disheveled, the faucet was facing the wrong way, the soap dish was askew, and there were noticeable water spots in the sink. (I promise I'm not obsessive...really!)

The first few times it caught my attention, I didn't say anything because I didn't want to nag at my husband. When I noticed my feelings were growing stronger, I decided to lovingly confront my husband.

I made sure I picked a time when neither of us were tired or stressed, and then I said, "You know, when I walk into the kitchen and things aren't exactly the way they're supposed to be, I feel like you don't love me...and our team is not winning. But when I walk into the kitchen and see everything done just right, I really feel like you love me...and our team does win."

I could have chosen to stew about it for weeks and then had a big blowup with my husband. Instead, I picked a strategic time when our emotions weren't running high and related our situation back to the "team win" concept. And because of that I was able to honestly communicate my feelings, and we both ended up laughing about the whole matter. After that we were able to move on and grow in our relationship with each other.

As we close out this chapter, I want to mention the most important principle to remember when facing conflict—above everything else, *let love always be your governing motivation*:

> Jesus replied: "'Love the Lord your God with all your heart and with all your soul and with all your mind.' This is the first and greatest commandment. And the second is like it: *'Love your neighbor as yourself.'*"[8]

> ...*speaking the truth in love*, we will grow to become in every respect the mature body of him who is the head, that is, Christ.[9]

So to sum it all up...Love God. Love people. That's it. Live by those rules, and you'll have mastered the art of peace.

Section 6

THE ART OF WAITING

*I'd like you to meet
my friend Carrie . . .*

$\mathcal{B}$EING A LADY-IN-WAITING during the Renaissance period sounds like a pretty sweet job! What's not to like about having a job that consists of hanging out, riding horses, reading love letters, and getting beauty treatments? I know, sign me up! It *probably* wasn't as glamorous as it sounds, and it was most certainly not awesome for the lady doing the waiting. We love to be *waited on* but almost universally despise the *act of waiting*. Think about it; no one likes waiting rooms. We're bored waiting in traffic or car pool lanes. We pray to never be on the waitlist for anything vital, and the list goes on. Granted, some of us are more patient than others, but it's fair to say our struggle with waiting is really about patience, and a lack of patience is rooted in our lack of trust.

Carrie Gant oversees the women's ministry at one of our campuses, and she wrote such a poignant chapter about the benefits of waiting on God as well as the pitfalls we can find ourselves in when we push ahead. Both Carrie and I came to know Jesus as our Lord when we were little girls and have been serving God ever since. I so appreciate how Carrie has determined to "see the beauty of the Lord in the land of the living." She recognizes God's faithfulness to her in every area of her life and seeks to encourage others to trust Him as well. On a less spiritual note, Carrie is my sugary snack sister! We're totally OK admitting that sugar runs through our veins.

Chapter Fourteen

PAUSE

Carrie Gant

Joy comes to us in moments—ordinary
moments. We risk missing out on joy when we
get too busy chasing down the extraordinary.[1]
BRENÉ BROWN

ARE YOU A good waiter?

I'm not talking about a waiter who serves food in
a restaurant. I'm talking about someone who's actively
waiting for something to happen.

So, let me ask you again: Are you a good waiter?

Are you content to live out each page of your life's
story one day at a time? Or do you feel as if you're
standing in the gate, chafing at the bit in your mouth
and raring to barrel ahead into whatever adventure
awaits you next?

It's so tempting to want to jump ahead to the

next chapter in our story. Living in the day to day of the here and now can often feel so monotonous and uneventful. We want to change the world...and we want to do it *now*.

When we can't clearly see what's ahead of us, many of us tend to feel anxious, and so we rush into projects and opportunities God never intended for us.

As hard as it may be to accept, the truth is, *you don't need to know the end of God's story for you; you just need to obey today. And sometimes that means hitting pause and waiting.*

I completely understand that waiting isn't so easy. I have a hard time waiting for the cookies to bake in the oven when I'm fixing them. On many occasions I've given in and eaten the raw cookie dough even though I know it's not good for me. I also know if I'll just wait a few minutes for them to bake in the oven, that what will come out is so very yummy, warm, and gooey. But even knowing all that doesn't stop me from enjoying the cookies before they're done, although they're not as satisfying as they could be. However, I *am* trying to get better at waiting for the right time.

And that's how God—the Author of our story— intended for it to be. Sometimes, yes, He *does* give us a little sneak peek at what He has in store for us, and when He does, we have to learn to wait and not make it happen on our own.

That's a lesson Sarah had to learn over the length of

her life, and it's a valuable lesson we can learn from her story as well.

The Book of Genesis is our primary source for all the details about Sarah's story. She was the wife of Abram and was originally born with the name Sarai, but God later changed her name to Sarah and his name to Abraham. (She was also Abram's half-sister, which seems incredibly inappropriate to us nowadays but was fairly common in tightly knit cultures back then.) When Sarai was about sixty-five years old, she and Abram left the land of Haran where they had lived their entire lives and headed out for an unknown land where God was leading them. They left behind most of their family and relatives and chose to believe God's promise to give them a multitude of descendants, even though at sixty-five and seventy-five they were childless.

Fast-forward ten years. Sarai is now seventy-five and Abram is eighty-five...still no kids in sight. God once again speaks to Abram and reaffirms His promise to give him and Sarai more descendants than they could ever count. At this point in time Sarai still desperately wants to believe God's promise, but she's not so sure about her ability to even have a baby because of her age. So she decides to help God out a little by taking matters into her own hands:

> Now Sarai, Abram's wife, had not been able to bear children for him. But she had an Egyptian servant named Hagar. So Sarai said

to Abram, "The Lord has prevented me from having children. Go and sleep with my servant. Perhaps I can have children through her." And Abram agreed with Sarai's proposal. So Sarai, Abram's wife, took Hagar the Egyptian servant and gave her to Abram as a wife. (This happened ten years after Abram had settled in the land of Canaan.)

So Abram had sexual relations with Hagar, and she became pregnant. But when Hagar knew she was pregnant, she began to treat her mistress, Sarai, with contempt. Then Sarai said to Abram, "This is all your fault! I put my servant into your arms, but now that she's pregnant she treats me with contempt. The Lord will show who's wrong—you or me!"

Abram replied, "Look, she is your servant, so deal with her as you see fit." Then Sarai treated Hagar so harshly that she finally ran away.[2]

Sarai wanted to have kids *so* badly. She figured if she couldn't be the one to physically give birth to them herself, then she'd just have to get a little creative. Plus, God wasn't exactly moving things forward, so she came up with a *foolproof* plan. (I mean what could *possibly* go wrong with offering up another woman to sleep with your husband so she'll get pregnant?)

What really went wrong is that Sarai grew weary of *waiting*.

I can so identify with Sarai. I know what it feels like to hear something from the Lord and then have to sit and wait. For most of my adult life I've felt like I was supposed to be involved in ministry; I just wasn't really sure the exact area of ministry where the Lord wanted me. Although to be perfectly honest, women's ministry was near the bottom of my list. I live in a house full of guys—a hubby, three teenage boys, and a male dog. I am definitely outnumbered. I got a horrible head-ache during the very first women's retreat I attended. I used to jokingly say it was because my body wasn't used to all the estrogen in the room. But even though it wasn't my passion, the Lord kept bringing women to me. So I finally got to the place where I was like, "OK, Lord...I get it. You want me to work with women."

I've had the privilege of knowing Debbie Morris for quite a while now. In fact, I met her during one of our first visits to Gateway more than thirteen years ago. Once I knew God wanted me to work with women, I could have easily gone to Pastor Debbie and tried to manipulate my way onto her team. (Although she is *way* too smart for that, so I know it wouldn't have worked on her.) But I didn't choose to go down that road. Instead, I learned from Sarai and decided to wait on the Lord and allow *Him* to promote me—and in His time He did. I've now been serving under Debbie's leadership for a little over a year, and I feel so honored to be a part of ministering to the women of Gateway Church. And through this entire journey the Lord has taught me that when I'm willing to wait on Him and humble myself, I get to see what I'm made of and grow in the process.

How many times does God say something to you, and even though you so desperately *want* to believe, when you don't see it happening as quickly as you think it should, you decide to step out and make something happen on your own? I confess it's happened to me *way* too many times. And then, when it inevitably doesn't turn out the way I thought it should, I—just like Sarai—get upset and angry with God and start to despise the very thing I've set in motion.

Sarai's master plan didn't end up looking quite as ideal as she'd pictured, and so her heart began to harden and she became bitter toward Abram and Hagar.

But then God spoke to Abram yet again:

> Then God said to him, "This is my covenant with you: I will make you the father of a multitude of nations! What's more, I am changing your name. It will no longer be Abram. Instead, you will be called Abraham, for you will be the father of many nations. I will make you extremely fruitful. Your descendants will become many nations, and kings will be among them! I will confirm my covenant with you and your descendants after you, from

generation to generation. This is the ever-lasting covenant: I will always be your God and the God of your descendants after you...."

Then God said to Abraham, "Regarding Sarai, your wife—her name will no longer be Sarai. From now on her name will be Sarah. And I will bless her and give you a son from her! Yes, I will bless her richly, and she will become the mother of many nations. Kings of nations will be among her descendants."

Then Abraham bowed down to the ground, but he laughed to himself in disbelief. "How could I become a father at the age of 100?" he thought. "And how can Sarah have a baby when she is ninety years old?" So Abraham said to God, "May Ishmael live under your special blessing!"

But God replied, "No—Sarah, your wife, will give birth to a son for you. You will name him Isaac, and I will confirm my covenant with him and his descendants as an everlasting covenant. As for Ishmael, I will bless him also, just as you have asked. I will make him extremely fruitful and multiply his descendants. He will become the father of twelve princes, and I will make him a great nation. But my covenant will be confirmed with Isaac, who will be born to you and Sarah about this time next year."[3]

God's telling Abram and Sarai once again that they're going to be the ancestors of many nations. Then God changed their names. Whenever God changes someone's name in the Bible, it's significant because it either relates to a character change or a major call from God. Abram's name is changed to Abraham; he went from "Exalted Father" to "Father of a Multitude." Sarai's name is changed to Sarah, and while both names mean the same—"Princess"—this new name serves to bring her into God's covenant in her own right.

At this point Sarah has a glimmer of hope that this promise is actually going to happen. She's moved from wanting to believe God's story for her to trying to write it on her own, and now she's ready to receive whatever God has in store for her.

Sarah opened up her heart to believe God again, and even though she was *ninety years old*, she chose to wait and trust that God was going to do what He said He would do. She'd learned a great deal from her past mistake of attempting to accomplish on her own something that was never her responsibility in the first place.

Because I can sometimes be a slow learner, the Lord regularly gives me opportunities to "practice" waiting. He'll often ask me to tell Him something that I would like to have—like maybe a great pair of shoes or piece of jewelry. Just recently I wanted a new purse, one of those fashionable designer ones that everyone seems to have. The Lord asked me to be very specific in my request and tell Him the color, style, and even price of what I wanted. So I willingly made my request known to Him. I'd like to say that I forgot about it after that or that I chose to sit back and wait patiently, but I really didn't. Each time I'd visit one of my favorite discount stores, I wondered if that would be the day and place I'd find my treasure. Sometimes the Lord has me wait for a few days; other times I wait for weeks or months. But the waiting is never in vain because I know He's told me that I will find it. Anyway, not too long after I asked the Lord about my purse, my husband and I were out on a date when I asked if we could stop by a store. I felt the Lord tell me to go in and look. So I walked in, looked around a bit, and there it was...color, check; style, check; and price, check. SCORE!

Doesn't that sound like so much fun! I've had several opportunities like this to practice waiting on the Lord, and it's not always with such a fun reward at the end. Some of my waiting has been very painful. However, I know God lets me go through those painful seasons of waiting so that when the harder, bigger things come and I have to wait even longer, I won't get discouraged as easily because I know He'll come through.

God is *always* faithful, and waiting on what He has, as Sarah learned, is so much better than anything you can come up with on your own. And once Sarah accepted that God's timing is always perfect (even when it's super hard to understand) and was *ready to receive*, she was *able to conceive* and see God's promise for her story fulfilled:

> The LORD kept his word and did for Sarah exactly what he had promised. She became pregnant, and she gave birth to a son for Abraham in his old age. This happened at just the time God had said it would. And Abraham named their son Isaac.[4]

When I first started to study this story, I thought Sarah had to conceive first and *then* receive her son—her promise. But God showed me that Sarah had to *receive* His promise before she could *conceive* her son. When Sarah finally was open to God and His perfect ways and timing, He blessed her with the deepest desire of her heart.

This is something God wants us to learn as well—the lesson is that there's so much beauty to be found in surrendering and peace to experience in waiting.

Has God given you a dream or spoken something to you and you're waiting for it to happen? *Don't give up. And don't rush ahead.*

I urge to take some time to examine your own heart. Ask the Holy Spirit to show you if there's something that you've been upset with Him about. Is there an expectation that hasn't been realized yet? A dream or promise that hasn't come to pass yet?

Whatever He brings to mind—no matter how small

it seems—release it to God, ask Him to forgive you for being impatient with His timing, and then open up your heart to Him again. Choose to believe, receive, and conceive whatever God promises to you.

Then just wait…and watch God's hand write far greater things into your story than you could ever imagine!

Section 7

LEARNING TO SEE

*I'd like you to meet
my friend Chelsea...*

IF YOU HAD to lose one of your senses, which one would it be? I would hate to lose my hearing or my taste buds; not being able to smell sounds dangerous, but the thought of not being able to see is probably the scariest for most of us. We couldn't drive, walk, or even read on our own anymore. We rely on our eyesight for everything from the practical to the emotional; we even talk about our spiritual *eyes*. Clearly, being able to see is important. Along with our actual vision, our perspective shapes everything we do, think, feel, and say. So is it reasonable to say that even if you have perfect eyesight, you must also address your perspective if you want to have a healthy, holistic view of life?

I certainly think so! The next several chapters are written by a friend of mine. I'm excited for you to meet her in these pages and hopefully come to appreciate her the way we do. *Sassy, spunky,* and *spectacular* are very fitting words to describe Chelsea Seaton, who joined our team in 2009. She spent some time as my assistant, among *many* other things, and now oversees the women's ministry at one of our campuses. I'm so proud of her! Chelsea is known for her humor and candor as well as her ability to make anyone feel like a friend.

Prepare to learn about the value of a healthy perspective and how blind spots and memory loss can block your ability to see God's hand working in your life and even cause you to doubt His goodness. Chelsea uses humor and personal stories to illustrate for us how easy it can be for God-loving people to have tunnel vision and how necessary it is to surround yourself with a few quality friendships you can count on in tough times. Finally, she gives us practical tips to be able to see like a hawk. I laughed out loud reading this, and I hope you will too!

Chapter Fifteen

VANTAGE POINT

Chelsea Seaton

What you see and what you hear depends a
great deal on where you are standing. It also
depends on what sort of person you are.[1]
C. S. Lewis

$\mathcal{B}$ACK IN 2008 I saw a movie titled *Vantage Point*
about the attempted assassination of a fictional Amer-
ican president. It wasn't (in my humble opinion) a great
movie, and I'll probably never watch it again. But I do
have to say the narrative approach the film took struck
me as pretty unique. Basically they repeated the same
twenty-three minutes of the events surrounding the
assassination attempt over and over again, but each
time those of us in the audience saw it from the perspective of a different character. Based on the "vantage

point" of the various characters, the story adds more and more clues until the whole picture becomes clear.

Isn't that kind of how real life is, though? Every story is told from a vantage point, and *your* vantage point—or perspective—determines how clearly you see each scene of your story. Obviously you're smack-dab in the middle of *your* story, so you can't see every single detail and component of what's actually happening in your life, but God can. Your vantage point is limited; His vantage point is limitless—He knows every single character, every single element, every single detail…past, present, and future.

But even though the scope of your perspective is finite, that doesn't mean it's irrelevant.

The truth, in fact, is quite the opposite—*your perspective is immensely influential in shaping the direction of your life.*

I truly believe one of the most important things you can do on a daily basis is shift your perspective. When our perspective is askew, we tend to head off in the wrong direction. But when we get our perspective in line with God's, our attitudes follow and subsequently our actions do as well.

Let me give you an example of this in my own life.

I work in the women's ministry department at my church. Every year we hold an awesome conference just for women, and I get to help plan and prepare for it. One year we ordered pretty charm bracelets to give away as gifts during the conference. When they arrived, I saw they all came packaged in a little bag, and I thought, "Great! They look so good, and I don't have to do anything else to them. We can give them away just like they are."

But then the rest of my team saw the bags and were like, "Uh, that's not gonna work. We need some ribbon and some tulle, and we need to make sure all those charm bracelets are in a much prettier package." I just stared at them in confusion and asked, "Why? They already came prepackaged, and plus, they look pretty enough to me as is." (Just a little FYI so you understand my confusion: I'm not really what you would call a "girly girl." I'm closer to what many women would consider a tomboy.)

Needless to say, I was overruled, and I was assigned the task of ordering green ribbon. Not necessarily a super daunting or complicated job, but it sure felt like it to me, because that is *not* my area of expertise. So, naturally, I started the arduous process of actually *selecting* what kind of green ribbon would work best. Once I cleared that hurdle, I had to figure out exactly how much ribbon to order.

Now, the other thing you need to know about me to fully understand this little story is that "math" and I are more like casual acquaintances than friends. We may occasionally run into each other from time to time, but there's no familiarity or instant connection. (In fourth grade I had to take a "modified math" class, OK?) And in this particular case we kind of moved from the casual acquaintance zone into the hostile enemy zone.

I tested some different lengths of ribbon on one of the bags and determined we needed around one foot of green ribbon per bag. Since I could only order in yards, I had to then figure out how many feet are in a yard. (By the way, there are three feet in a yard...you can store that little tidbit of info in your mind palace just in case you need it for future reference when your life is on the line.) I knew we had 4,000 charm bracelets, so that meant we needed 4,000 feet of green ribbon, which came out to about 1,350 yards. I found out there were a thousand yards of ribbon on each spool, so I did some quick calculations in my head and decided I needed to order four spools. (I know, I know...*way* too much ribbon for what we needed. But I didn't know that *then*.)

OK, here's where the story takes a twist. The week before the conference the boxes of ribbon finally came...and came...and came.

Turns out, I hadn't ordered *four* spools of ribbon; I had ordered *forty*! For those of you who are math challenged like me, that means we had twelve thousand feet of green ribbon. Oh, and did I forget to mention the order was nonreturnable and nonrefundable?

In that moment when I realized what had happened, I immediately had to make a choice. I could look at all those boxes and boxes and boxes of green ribbon and bemoan the fact that this kind of disaster "*always* happens to me." I could think, "I'm horrible at my job. I've just wasted so much of the church's money. I can't believe I did this; I'm so stupid!"

Or I could look at all that green ribbon and say, "Well, I made a mistake. That happens to everyone from time to time. And now? We have enough green ribbon for the next twelve years. Guess I need to find some ways for us to use it all."

I chose to respond the second way.

If I'd chosen to view the situation from a vantage point of defeat or failure, every time I prepared for an event from that point on, I would have struggled with so much insecurity. Every time I needed to order something or do a little math, I'd worry about screwing up. My peace and confidence in who I am and my talents would be overshadowed by a simple mistake I'd made once. I'd be paralyzed into inaction and doubt.

Perspective is all in how you look at it.

Poor perspective sees misfortune; healthy perspective sees opportunities.

Over the next several chapters we're going to look at the blind spots that poor perspective creates and then discover where we can go to get a healthy perspective.

Chapter Sixteen

AMNESIA

Chelsea Seaton

God isn't an editor; He's a creator. He's
not looking for the typos in our lives;
He's looking for the beauty in them.[1]
BOB GOFF

WITHOUT WASTING ANY time, let's jump right
into identifying the four different blind spots created
by poor perspective, shall we?

The very first blind spot is memory loss. When bad
perspective starts creeping in, it limits your ability to
see clearly. So when you try and look back at your past
experiences, you only see the bad; all of a sudden you
forget every good thing God has done up to this point.

It's like selective amnesia seizes our consciousness
and blurs out the countless times and ways God has
proved His faithfulness in our lives. You get a phone

call with bad news, and instantly you forget that three days before God moved powerfully on your behalf and knocked down an obstacle staring you straight in the face. You forget His love for you and all the amazing things He's already done and provided for you, because you have short-term memory loss.

I know I definitely experience this kind of memory loss from time to time. My roommate and I love each other like sisters, but occasionally we'll also fight like sisters. Most of the time we'll be arguing over the dumbest and most insignificant thing, and the first thought that pops into my mind is, "This is awful! We've been arguing SO MUCH lately!" Now, mind you, we probably have one quick little five-minute fight every six months or so, but when I'm in the middle of it, I'm convinced we fight all the time. In that moment I just *know* she's annoyed with me, doesn't love me anymore, and wants to move out tomorrow.

You'd think I start to wonder if I'm going just a little bit crazy when I have insanely irrational thoughts like that—except I know I'm not alone in this. The Israelites were struck with a sudden onset of short-term memory loss when they reached the Red Sea mere days after being freed from their enslavement in Egypt. If you're a little fuzzy on the details of the story, let me give you a quick refresher.

For years and years the Israelites had cried out to God to deliver them from their captivity to the Egyptians. They pleaded, "God, please send someone...*anyone*...to set us free." Suddenly Moses appears on the scene, and he's confronting Pharaoh—the supreme ruler over all of Egypt—and demanding that the people be let go. Pharaoh scoffs at what he views as Moses's request but, in actuality, is a command from God—the Supreme Ruler and Creator of *the world*. So God sends plague after plague to devastate the Egyptians' livestock, land, and lives, but God spares the Israelites from experiencing any awful effects from the plagues. Even when death visits every household in the land of Egypt, God provides a way of escape for the Israelites. And then? God sets them free! They gather up all their stuff and leave the country of their captivity. As they're praising and thanking God for delivering them, they reach the Red Sea and realize Pharaoh's regretted his decision to release them. Now he's chasing after them with his entire army of men, horses, and chariots—and all the amazing, unbelievable miracles they've *just seen* vanishes from their memories. It's like the entire nation of Israelites is collectively and instantly plagued by amnesia.

They start panicking and moaning: "We're all gonna die! Moses, did you make us follow you here just so we could get massacred? Weren't the graves back in Egypt good enough? You should have left us alone and never bothered us." They forgot all the thousands of prayers they'd prayed for deliverance.

I wonder how many times we're right on the verge of seeing God prove His faithfulness to us one more time, but we start worrying, panicking, and moaning like the Israelites. They were just moments away from witnessing the Red Sea part and seeing God prove His faithfulness.

I know I personally struggle with this type of memory loss when I experience some bad news and start thinking insane (and untrue) thoughts such as: "I think God's punishing me. That has to be it. That's why this awful thing is happening to me right now." I don't know if you ever have thoughts like that, but I usually start to mentally rehash all the ways I've sinned or been unfaithful. And then I buy into the lie that God's faithfulness to me is somehow contingent on my faithfulness to Him.

If you can relate, let me tell you something about God that we need to hear and remind ourselves of over and over again: *God is a good dad.*

God is not going to shove you out in the middle of the street so you'll learn how to watch out for cars. Do you know any mom who would say to her daughter, "OK, honey. We're gonna learn all about cars today. So I want you to stand right there in center of the street, and you go get 'em, slugger!" No! Of course not! If we saw a mom doing that to her child, we'd probably either ream her out or report her to our local child protection agency. (I'd most likely do both.) So why do we believe God would do something like that to us?

Do you think God is watching you with a naughty-or-nice list and saying, "Well, Jennifer was unfaithful to Me that one time in 2007, so now I think it's time for her to learn her lesson. Oh, I know! Let's drop her there in the middle of that busy highway and see if she can navigate herself out of that mess!" How ridiculous is that? But we let our poor perspective cloud our memories of God's faithfulness, just as the Israelites did at the Red Sea.

The reality is God's holding your hand the whole time, saying, "Hey, don't run out into the street by yourself, OK? There's nothing good for you there. Cars are flying by left and right, and I don't want you to get hit. Here, take this…it's the book I've written for you so you'll be able to watch out for cars heading straight at you and get out of the way safely."

And even when you do run out into the middle of the street on your own—whether thoughtlessly or willfully—God still doesn't abandon you. Even though He didn't get you into the mess, He's going to get you out. He rescues us time and time again.

Why? *Because His faithfulness has nothing to do with your faithfulness.*

Remembering *that* is the first step to eliminating blind spots in your perspective.

Chapter Seventeen

ASSUME NOTHING

Chelsea Seaton

> You have to choose to get rid of the toxic
> and get back in alignment with God. You
> can be overwhelmed by every small
> setback in life, or you can be energized
> by the possibilities they bring.[1]
> CAROLINE LEAF

OUR FIRST BLIND spot was memory loss…but there are still three more yet to come. So let's move on to our second one.

Poor perspective also creates *the blind spot of assumptions*. And I think the number one incorrect assumption is this: God has forgotten me.

We have thoughts like:

- "Why isn't my husband like that lady's husband? He serves in so many ways at church and seems like such an attentive and loving husband. He even takes her out on a date once a week...WITHOUT their kids! What did I do to deserve the man I ended up with, God? Have You forgotten little ol' me down here?"

- "Her kids are all so well behaved and playing together nicely. Look, that one's even reading her Bible! I have no idea where my kids are...probably running around like banshees. God, why can't my kids be better behaved? I'm so worn out from always having to discipline them, and NOTHING seems to work. I'm pleading with You, God...when are You going to answer me?"

- "God, I look around me, and ALL of my girlfriends are getting married. Scratch that...they're already all married. And now they're starting to have babies, while I haven't even been on a date in two years! I've been praying for a godly husband for a long time here...are You even hearing me anymore?"

If you've ever felt this way or wondered these kinds of questions, know this: you're not alone. The other thing I want you to know is this: *God is always working on your behalf.*

Don't believe me? That's OK. Let me show you what God's Word says about it:

> Come and see what God has done, the amazing things he has done for people.[2]

> Since ancient times no one has heard, no ear has perceived, no eye has seen any God besides you, who acts on behalf of those who wait for him.[3]

> And we know that in all things God works for the good of those who love him, who have been called according to his purpose.[4]

If you've surrendered your life to God's control, then you've been "called according to his purpose," and He is always working on your behalf.

I'm twenty-eight years old and single. Now, I think I'm still young and have time to meet someone and get married. But I'm *constantly* asked if I'm dating. When my answer is often no, the immediate follow-up question is usually: "Well, are you putting yourself out there?" (And what on earth does that even *mean*?)

I could choose to look at my singleness and cry about it. I could focus solely on the fact that I'm not dating—and not only am I not dating, but I also don't have a single (male) prospect in sight.

Or I could dwell on the truth and trust that *God is always working on my behalf.* And right now, wherever my husband is, God is working on his behalf too while also working in him…just as He's working in me. The Holy Spirit is molding and shaping him while working things out of him so he'll be ready to meet me. At the same time, God is molding and shaping me, while working things out of me, so I'll be ready to meet him.

If you're reading this right now and you're single and it seems like all hope is lost, I'm here to tell you that hope is working for you right now! God is a God of hope, and He's working and molding and shaping and doing more than you could ever see or know. It's your job as a follower of God to stand on the promise that He is working for you.

So what should we do when a bad situation or circumstance happens and we assume that God's forgotten us? That's when we choose to look past the blind spot of memory loss and *remember* all the countless times when God has been faithful to us. And you never know; the situation you're in right now could be the very thing God uses to propel you into the purpose He's called you to.

I've had some rough times in my life. I could sit down with you and talk for hours about the attacks my family has undergone. We've been in situations that seemed to have no end in sight. But you know what?

I wouldn't trade it one bit, because in those seemingly hopeless situations, God has always proved His faithfulness to me.

I'm telling you: your horrible situation could very well be your Red Sea moment when God shows up powerfully, does a miraculous work, and leads you through a figurative raging sea on dry land.

One of my personal favorite heroines is the late Corrie ten Boom. She was an incredible godly woman who survived the Holocaust and wrote several books about how she and her family hid Jews from the Nazis. In her book *The Hiding Place* she said:

> Every experience God gives us, every person
> He puts in our lives is the perfect preparation
> for the future that only He can see.[5]

I love that! If you had the tiniest inkling of just how much God loves and cares for you, there would be little room for doubt about His faithfulness to creep in.

Never ever forget…God is always, always, always working on your behalf.

Chapter Eighteen

TUNNEL VISION

Chelsea Seaton

If you look the right way, you can see
that the whole world is a garden.[1]
FRANCES HODGSON BURNETT

*T*HE THIRD BLIND spot poor perspective creates is *tunnel vision*—where you're unable to see the big picture because you can only see what's right in front of you face.

Tunnel vision is the tendency to focus only on a single or limited point of view, and this is probably the blind spot I'm most susceptible to getting caught off guard by.

When I allow myself to develop a poor perspective, tunnel vision hits me straight between the eyes and blocks what I can see. I can't see anything but myself and whatever problem I'm dealing with at the time.

Tunnel vision makes me think my problem is all there is and limits my ability to see the bigger picture.

My mom and roommate can attest to what I'm about to share with you, but I have a serious problem with tunnel vision when it comes to things in my house. I had it when I lived with my mom, and I still have it now living on my own.

I don't know what it is, but the moment I step through the door of my home, something comes over me. When I open up the refrigerator door and look for milk, I can't find it anywhere. I promise you...it is *nowhere* to be found. But then my roommate walks up to the fridge, removes the carton of orange juice in the way, and *voila!* There's the milk!

I secretly think she and my mom are in cahoots with one another, because when I was growing up, I'd *always* lose something in the laundry. I'd search and search and search, but I could never find it.

Finally I'd say, "Mom! I can't find my softball uniform. It's gone!"

And she'd respond, "It's in your closet, Chels."

Convinced I was right, I'd say, "No, it's not. It's *gone.*"

Once again she'd say, "I'm positive it's in your closet with all your other clean clothes."

"Maybe you didn't wash it. Mom, you know I have a game today, and I need a clean uniform. What am I gonna do?"

And then my mom would walk into my room, go to my closet, and move a coat out of the way, and lo and behold—there was my softball uniform hanging, clean as could be.

So tunnel vision is an issue for me because all I can see is what's *directly* in front of my face.

We do that with our prayers all the time. We approach God with just one thing on our mind:

- "O Lord, I want to get married. I want to get married so bad. Let me get married. I just want to get married."

- "God, my marriage is broken. Please fix my marriage. My marriage is on the rocks. I need You to fix my marriage. My marriage is broken."

- "Father, I really need healing. Will You heal me? Please heal me, God! I need healing! I need You to move and heal me, Lord!"

That's tunnel vision at full effect in our prayers. Nothing else seems to matter.

When this happens, you have to take a step back and try to see the big picture. Because sometimes I'm the orange juice or the coat that needs to be moved out the way in order for the bigger picture to become clear.

And there *is* a bigger picture. It's bigger than you and bigger than me. You may look at your kids, and it seems like they're not following God at all. But He's working on their story, just as He's working on yours.

God has you, your kids, your friends, your spouse, and your family securely in His hands. He's protecting them and has it all under control. There's a much bigger picture here at work that only He knows.

Chapter Nineteen

BETTER TOGETHER

Chelsea Seaton

The *I* in illness is isolation, and the
crucial letters in wellness are *we*.
AUTHOR UNKNOWN

THE FINAL BLIND spot created by poor perspective
is *isolation*.

When memory loss happens, we forget God's faithfulness. When we give in to assumptions, we forget
God's always working on our behalf. When tunnel
vision is present, we can only see our problems and fail
to see there's a much bigger picture that God is in control of.

But when you let poor perspective create a sense
of isolation in you, that's when the devil has you right
where he wants you. He knows that when you're alone,
he can influence you the most.

Let me explain. Whenever you're vulnerable with someone else, it immediately diminishes the devil's ability to influence you. The second you confess your struggle with poor perspective, it gets exposed to light. And just as when you flip on a light switch, any darkness disappears.

Every time you choose to be vulnerable and open about your struggles, the results are immediate—darkness loses whatever stranglehold it has on you. That's why you need to write it down in your journal or tell your spouse, a friend, a counselor, a pastor. *Whatever* you need to do, make sure you get it out. Expose it to the light.

Sometimes I'll have the most ridiculous thoughts; for instance, I'll start convincing myself I'm never going to get married…like ever! Then I start thinking, "I have nothing to offer. Oh, woe is me!" But when I finally mention it to a friend after dwelling on it for a week or two, she'll immediately step in and help me get my perspective straightened out. Plus, whenever I start talking aloud about my crazy thoughts to her, I start to realize how ridiculous they sound.

That's why I so strongly believe it's absolutely imperative to have trustworthy people in your life who are actively seeking the Lord and whom you can talk to.

Journaling is also an important step for me. When I start writing down my thoughts and then come back to them after a while, I'm able to clearly spot the lies I'd believed and realize I was seeing and hearing through a wrong filter.

As long as you stay isolated with your poor perspective, then one assumption turns into another assumption, which turns into another. The longer you stay isolated, the more prone you are to memory loss and the harder it is to walk out of it.

Isolation is a scary, scary place to be. That's why so many movies, TV shows, and books portray solitary confinement as the *worst* possible punishment. At all costs, don't inadvertently let yourself get into a place of isolation...and certainly don't choose it.

Understand, however, that there's a difference between solitude and isolation. Solitude can be refreshing and much needed for your soul. The Bible tells us that Jesus, on numerous occasions, went off by Himself to pray and spend time with His Father, and we're called to follow His example. Wayne Cordeiro says:

> Solitude is a chosen separation for refining your soul. Isolation is what you crave when you neglect the first.[1]

When you sense yourself starting to feel isolated from everyone else, resist the devil's attempt to trap you. Confront the lies he's whispering to you that make you feel shame and condemnation. And then don't let him get the upper hand. Immediately go and talk to someone. Whether it's face-to-face, on the phone, or through an e-mail or text, just be honest with *someone*. Don't wait for isolation to surround you. Expose your struggle to the light. Let it out so it can't morph or grow into anything else.

The Bible tells us:

> Therefore confess your sins to each other and
> pray for each other so that you may be healed.
> The prayer of a righteous person is powerful
> and effective.[2]

This verse is saying that when you confess your struggle or your sins to another person who follows Jesus, you may experience healing—it could be physical, mental, or emotional. Do you realize that the people in your life are not there by coincidence? Maybe God put a specific person in your life just so they would be there to hear what you have to say, to help you see the big picture, and to remind you of His faithfulness. Remember, God is *always* working on your behalf— and that includes the people He surrounds you with.

Chapter Twenty

SUPERNATURAL
PERSPECTIVE

If you take your Bible and pray, "Lord, I am blind
without You. I can't understand the Bible unless
You show me," then He will open your spiritual
eyes, and things will begin to jump off the page.[1]
ROBERT MORRIS

A PERSON WITH 20/20 vision is considered to have
normal vision.

The 20/20 part means *your* ability to see detail at
twenty feet is the same as the ability of someone else
who has normal eyesight to see detail from twenty feet
away.

If you were to have 20/40 vision, then you would
have to be twenty feet away from an object to see it
as clearly as someone with normal eyesight could see it

standing forty feet away. If you were standing forty feet from the object, you would only see it half as well as someone with normal eyesight.

The best vision a person could possibly hope to achieve with the naked human eye is 20/8. But certain birds, like hawks, can actually see at a 20/2 level! (Coincidentally I used to be my high school's mascot...and would you believe we were the Hawks?)

That's the kind of vision we should seek to have—not with our physical eyes, of course; I'm talking about our spiritual perspective.

Think about it...20/20 is considered "normal" vision right? So shouldn't we want our spiritual perspective to be far greater than normal?

We can't achieve this kind of supernatural perspective on our own; it's beyond our ability. But when we submit our perspective to the Holy Spirit and ask Him to help us see the world through His eyes, we're able to see better than normal. We're able to see with what I call a 20/2 perspective.

If you want to know how to gain this kind of incredible perspective, you have to first know where it *doesn't* come from. Healthy perspective never ever comes from comparison. A lot of times people try to shift their perspective by comparing where they are to where someone else is. When I hear someone say, "Well, it could be a whole lot worse, so I better get over it," I think that's just ridiculous. That comparison isn't based on any of God's promises for your life; it's based in shame and

condemnation (which the Bible says come from Satan).
The Bible *does* say:

> Each person should judge his own actions and
> *not compare himself with others*. Then he can
> be proud for what he himself has done. Each
> person must be responsible for himself.[2]

God has a specific plan for you, only you, so there's
no point in comparing your life to anyone else's...none.
We're going to go over the trap of comparison pretty
thoroughly in the next few chapters, but suffice it to
say, if you want a healthy perspective, steer clear of
comparison.

Now, do you want to know *how* you can get 20/2
perspective?

You go to the number-one best-selling book of
all time—the Bible. When you're caught up in your
memory loss, that's the book that will remind you of
God's faithfulness. It's where you'll discover words of
truth and words of love:

> The LORD is compassionate and gracious,
> slow to anger, abounding in love. He will
> not always accuse, nor will he harbor his
> anger forever; he does not treat us as our sins
> deserve or repay us according to our iniquities.
> For as high as the heavens are above the earth,
> so great is his love for those who fear him;
> as far as the east is from the west, so far has

he removed our transgressions from us. As a
father has compassion on his children, so the
LORD has compassion on those who fear him;
for he knows how we are formed, he remem-
bers that we are dust.[3]

Has your mind or the devil lied to you and made
you think God's not for you? Do you feel like God has
forgotten you? Turn to God's Word. From Genesis to
Revelation the Bible tells us the story of God's faithfulness and lets us know He's always working on our
behalf:

Understand, therefore, that the LORD your
God is indeed God. He is the faithful God
who keeps his covenant for a thousand generations and lavishes his unfailing love on those
who love him and obey his commands.[4]

And if you take the time to immerse yourself in its
pages and ask the Holy Spirit to reveal its truth to you,
the Bible will help you see the bigger picture of how
God is redeeming the world through those of us who
follow Him. You'll discover how He's bringing people
to Him, how He's healing people, and how He wants
to heal you and bring you nearer to Him:

O LORD my God, you have performed many
wonders for us. Your plans for us are too
numerous to list. You have no equal. If I tried

> to recite all your wonderful deeds, I would never come to the end of them.[5]

When you're feeling isolated, alone, and trapped by loneliness, here's the double-edged sword that will pierce the darkness hovering over you:

> For the word of God is alive and powerful. It is sharper than the sharpest two-edged sword, cutting between soul and spirit, between joint and marrow. It exposes our innermost thoughts and desires.[6]

The Bible is your best friend, because it tells you all the things you need to hear to bring you back to what God has in store for you. And if you dig into the Bible, you'll see how God's promises are far bigger and greater than you could ever imagine! It is the key you need for *everything*. And this book—God's Word—is where 20/2 perspective comes from!

> By his divine power, God has given us everything we need for living a godly life. We have received all of this by coming to know him, the one who called us to himself by means of his marvelous glory and excellence.[7]

God gives us divine power through His Word and sends us on a treasure hunt of sorts where we learn stories throughout the Old Testament, parables in the

Gospels, principles laid out in Proverbs, commands from God, testimonies of the saints, and songs from the psalmists. They all weave together a magnificent tapestry that teaches us to start seeing how *He* sees and gives us a guide to conform our thinking, seeing, hearing, speaking, and believing to Him.

Our perspective is shaped much like a small child who learns either from her parents or from her teachers. *Our* primary teacher and parent is God Himself. When we stop looking to Him as the standard, we default into comparing ourselves with those around us. It's like taking a limp, cooked noodle and trying to use it as a straight edge for architectural drawings. It would be horrible! And yet when we take our eyes off of God, we use faulty measures on ourselves all the time.

So let's take a look at some of the most common pitfalls of comparison.

Section 8

AVOIDING THE COMPARISON TRAP

I'd like you to meet my friend Sandy . . .

$\mathcal{S}$HOPPING ONLINE IS so easy these days! You can go to special sites to find the product you want and simultaneously compare every aspect from price to weight, customer reviews to return policies. You can make an informed decision and feel like you're getting the best product for the best price. Comparison doesn't stop there, though, does it? We compare our cooking with that of others, and our holiday decorations with Facebook and Instagram friends, and oh, yeah, then there's Pinterest. Comparison can actually be paralyzing sometimes. Have you ever been stranded in the vitamin aisle trying to decipher ingredients while making the best choice based on your limited understanding of the contents? Me too. And it's exhausting!

My dear friend Sandy Jobe and I have talked a lot about this. Over the years a staggering number of methods for comparison have emerged! As if we haven't been struggling with this for centuries, now we can feel inadequate driving down the road or sitting in the privacy of our own homes. Sandy has been in some form of ministry her entire adult life, including her current role as a member of our team. She's known for being an excellent cook, while I'm known for being excellent at enjoying *other* people's cooking!

In the final few chapters of our book Sandy sets out to help us free ourselves from the trap of comparison and be loosed from the chains of fear, insecurity, and inferiority. She helps clarify how ability isn't the same as calling and that just as each of us is unique, so are the gifts, talents, and timing God has ordained for us. Finally she delves into our tendency to judge, both others and ourselves—and how if we label ourselves incorrectly, it leads straight to death; but if we do it correctly, according to God's Word, it leads to life.

Chapter Twenty-One

NO WIN IN COMPARISON

Sandy Jobe

> Don't determine where you are based on where
> anyone else is. There is no win in comparison.[1]
> ANDY STANLEY

ALL MY LIFE I've struggled with comparing myself to others. Several months ago I was invited to share at a women's event. After I accepted the invitation, the church hosting the event sent me a little informational packet with a brochure that highlighted all of the featured guests. When I saw who some of the other speakers were, I immediately felt paralyzed by fear and thought, "Oh, my! How can I tell them, 'Hey! I made a mistake'? I can't make it to this event. Those other speakers are WAY out of my league! They speak with such authority, and it just seems so easy for them."

Then I remembered, "Oh, yeah, I'm supposed to

speak about comparison at this event. I wonder if my fear has anything to do with this?"

Have you ever noticed that whenever you think you've mastered an area of weakness, you're most likely going to be tested in the very area you're trying to strengthen or change? As a mom I can't begin to count the number of times when my children were young and I told one of them to be kind, and then *two minutes later* I was faced with the opportunity to be kind myself.

So here I was getting ready to speak to a group of women about comparison and struggling to overcome it myself. I was comparing my abilities, or what I perceived to be lack of ability, with the other speakers. I was doubting God's calling on my life and feeling an overwhelmingly intense pressure to run away and hide. Comparison was sucking the life out of me.

But then God gently reminded me: "Sandy, all you have to do is share *your* story."

Yes, they were all incredibly gifted speakers, but God was trying to show me I wasn't *them* and He wanted to work through *me*...if I'd give Him the chance. I didn't have to share *their* story; I just had to share *mine*.

I've been married to a wonderful man since 1980. Together we've raised three incredible kids who are now adults, and we have the world's cutest grandson. This is a portion of *my* story. You might be single and fresh out of college or a recent retiree...regardless of what season of life you're in right now, your story is going to look uniquely different than the story of anyone else.

We each have our own story that's specific to us, and we're all on different pages of our stories. And yet we all fall into the trap of comparing ourselves to someone else.

We see another woman and think, "She looks so put together. If only I had her hair...*her looks...her clothes budget.*"

Every time I pick up a fashion magazine, I find myself wishing I had those eyes or wore that dress size or had smoother skin. According to what is constantly published as "The Look," NOTHING about me is right. In my heart I know nothing is further from the truth. Yet the voices are constantly speaking lies to try and tear us down.

Because our enemy is a deceiver, he whispers lie after lie to us in an effort to get us to forget who we are as daughters of God and doubt the truth about what He's deposited in us.

Sadly we all too often go along with the devil's lies and live as if they're really true. Rarely do we stop to ask, "Who's saying these things to me? Who's causing me to doubt myself? Is it me? Is there something from my past that led me to believe this? Or is it the enemy of my soul disguising his voice as my own?"

And do you know where it all started? That's right. At the very beginning. The devil's been trying to get us to step into the snare of comparison since the Garden of Eden. In the form of a serpent Satan essentially asked Eve, "Don't you want to be like God?"[2] He was trying to get her to believe the lie that she didn't measure up. Who God made her to be wasn't good enough. And the second Eve entertained the idea, she immediately began to doubt, which led to the sin and then, ultimately, death.

After Eve and Adam ate the fruit from the tree of the knowledge of good and evil, they started to feel inadequate, right? They realized they were naked. I've always wondered how they figured that out. I mean, there was no one else there in the garden whom they could compare themselves to.

God asked Eve and Adam, "Who told you that you were naked?"[3] And I believe He asked them that because He wanted them to be aware that those lies whispered in their hearts didn't come from Him; they came from their enemy who wanted to create a separation between them and God.

And from there it only got worse. Some years after Eve and Adam were kicked out of Eden, their two sons Abel and Cain picked up on their parents' comparison struggle—for sure, Cain did. He killed his brother Abel because he was jealous of how God accepted Abel's offering to Him and not his. His feeling of not measuring up led him to commit murder.

When you hear a voice in your head whispering, "You're fat. You're ugly. You're too short. You're too tall. You don't know how to speak. There's something wrong with you," I'm telling you that's *not* the Holy Spirit.

So the first thing you need to do is be aware. Know where the voice of comparison comes from.

When we turn comparison inward and focus on ourselves, it often causes us to withdraw and isolate. When we turn comparison outward, it often causes jealousy, which left untreated can lead to bitterness. That's why comparing yourself to anyone else is a bad idea.

In his second letter to the followers of Jesus who lived in Corinth, Paul makes his feelings about comparison pretty clear:

> Oh, don't worry; we wouldn't dare say that we are as wonderful as these other men who tell you how important they are! But they are only comparing themselves with each other, using themselves as the standard of measurement. How ignorant![4]

He's advising us in pretty black and white terms to learn from his example and stay away from comparison.

A few years ago I went to Italy with my sister. It was such an amazing opportunity and incredible trip. We went with a large group of people, and there were some really smart educators in the group.

One of the days we stepped into a beautiful, elegant hotel to have some coffee at the café there. As we were all walking through the lobby, we heard voices speaking English. So naturally we stopped, and we saw two couples from the States drinking coffee. As we struck up a conversation with them, one of the ladies mentioned where she had attended college, and it turned out there were several people in our group who attended the same school. That quickly led to a conversation about the different academic degrees everyone had earned. One lady had a master's degree, and another one had completed her doctorate. I just stood there thinking, "Man, all these people are so smart!"

Then one of the men sitting there zeroed in on me and asked, "And you, young lady, what do you have a degree in?" The instant he asked that question, I froze. The only thought racing through my mind was, "Don't you see all these other people standing here with me? Couldn't you have asked one of them? What am I going to tell him? I'm so stupid. I've never gotten a degree like all of these other women."

But I kept my cool and said, "Well, when I was nineteen, I got my MRS degree. And when I was twenty, I got my MOM degree. Then I started working on my PhT [putting hubby through college]. I've also been a full-time domestic engineer for thirty-four years and a full-time life coach."

That man looked at me and said, "Wow, a full-time life coach? What does that look like?"

I responded, "When you have three kids like I do, coaching them through life is a full-time job."

He laughed and said, "Young lady, that is amazing! Do you have a business card? Because you should!"

That was an opportunity for me to hang my head

and say, "I didn't go to college. I'm dumb." I chose, instead, to not give in to the lie of comparison.

But even as I was walking away from that conversation, comparison attacked me again. The thought flashed through my mind: "See, you should have gone to college. Now you're in your fifties, and you have nothing to fall back on if anything ever happens to your family." I let that thought linger for just a millisecond, and then I thought: "No, it was worth it for me to have all those years staying at home with my babies to raise them. It was worth it to go without and not have some of the nicer things my other friends did." But we never really lacked for anything important.

When my kids tell others about having a playhouse made out of cardboard, I used to get embarrassed and think, "Oh, I wish they wouldn't tell those stories!" But then I realized...you know what? They never knew the difference! They never thought they were missing out just because their playhouse was made out of refrigerator boxes their dad had put together for them. They thought it was awesome! My kids would cut windows out of their playhouse and create furniture on the walls with crayons and paint. They loved it, and it helped fashion who they are today. Now, when they do get wonderful things in life, they're appreciative, grateful, and excited about it.

Whenever you compare two things, you're essentially examining them to see what their similarities and differences are in order to measure their worth or significance. So when you compare yourself to someone else, you're rating your *worth* in relation to that person rather than God—the only true standard.

Allowing comparisons to influence any portion of your story can sow seeds of fear, insecurity, and a sense of inferiority. We know that at the core of each of these is an unhealthy or disproportionate focus on self—aka selfishness. If our eyes are fixed on ourselves, that means we've taken them off God and elevated our own opinions or those of others above God's. This sets us up for great disappointment, hurt, and even derailment from the story God wants to write for us. The bottom line is that we are fearfully and wonderfully made. In God's eyes we are created beyond comprehension. You simply cannot beat that comparison.

In the next chapter we'll take a look at how comparison robs you from living life to its fullest.

Chapter Twenty-Two

TAILOR MADE

Sandy Jobe

> You absolutely can have and do it all, and
> live the life you've dreamed of…if you
> understand that your "all" will be a journey of
> a lifetime, and that sometimes your "all" can
> shift and morph when you least expect it.[1]
> CHRISTINE CAINE

*G*OD CREATED YOU with a specific purpose in mind, and He's slowly maturing you to look more and more like Him—to be an expression of His image here on earth. When you compare yourself to anyone else, you short-circuit His process. You've taken your eyes off of Him and His Word, and you've started to look at others for your standard of measurement.

I really don't mean to sound harsh, but *comparison is basically the sin of idolatry.*

It's so easy to fall into this. We compare our bodies, our children, our spouses, our homes, our cars, our jobs, our finances, our looks, our hair, our clothes, God's favor, God's calling, His spiritual gifts, trials, and burdens. We even compare our journey in life. *When we start looking at anything or anyone other than God, we're focused on the wrong standard.*

Comparison can be especially destructive when it leads you to be critical and look down on others. That can often cause paralysis—first in you and then in the person you're criticizing. Let me ask you: Has criticism ever stopped *you* in your tracks and led you to believe you can't do something? Has it ever convinced you that someone else can do it (whatever "it" may be) way better than you can, so you shouldn't even give it a shot? OK, so if that's how criticism makes you feel, then it's also how someone being criticized by you is going to feel.

Several years ago I was in a small group, and the group leader asked all of us (ahead of time) to share about the most traumatic experience we'd ever had. I couldn't, for the life of me, figure out which one of the many horrible things I'd experienced in my life I should share about with the group. And so I made sure I wasn't the first one to share.

The lady who *did* go first started off by saying, "Wow, this was kind of a hard exercise!" My first thought was, "No kidding! I'm having such a hard time picking my MOST traumatic experience. Should I share about sexual abuse, my brain surgery, or the other ten surgeries I've had?" Then she continued, "I just grew up in the most amazing home. We never had any major conflict there." She just went on and on about how great her life was growing up. The more she talked, the more I started wondering, "God, what did I do to deserve all the awful things I've experienced in life?" I started feeling really sorry for myself. Finally I heard the lady say, "After thinking about what to share, I'm pretty sure one of the most traumatic experiences I've ever had is when I got called to the church nursery one time, because my daughter swallowed her tiny hair bow that had been stuck to her head with Karo Syrup."

I sat there in disbelief. *Really? Your child swallowed her tiny hair bow, and THAT is the most traumatic thing you've ever experienced?* I immediately began to compare my life with hers and feel superior, because my life had been so much worse. (Trust me, I know I was horrible for thinking that. Don't judge me; I'm just being honest.)

A few years ago I ran into that same lady at the mall. It had been so long since we'd talked, and I was so glad to see her and catch up a bit. Then she began to share with me a little bit about her journey and told me she was in the darkest time of her life—the deepest, darkest valley she'd ever been in. Standing there in the department store, she just started sobbing. I was immediately overcome with a tidal wave of empathy for my friend and conviction for my attitude from years before.

Later, as I slid into my car, my heart was still hurting

deeply. I prayed, "God, I'm so sorry I judged her so harshly. And all because she hadn't experienced what I had. I didn't think her trials were as 'bad' as mine."

And I felt God gently say, "Don't ever forget...when you want to trade places with someone, you'd have to trade their trials too. You'd have to exchange burdens with them as well."

You may feel like you're in a pit right now, and you're looking at someone else and it doesn't seem like she's in as bad a spot as you. But you have no idea. Her life may not be anywhere near as good or glamorous as it looks. You can't make a judgment call based on what little you can see in someone else.

Our job is to say, "God, You've made me. You've called me. And You've equipped me. You promised me that You know the plans You have for me, and those plans are to give me a future and a hope. So I'm asking You to help me learn how to be content with where You have me right now and give me the grace to climb the mountain before me."

Sometimes we take comparison a step beyond just identifying what's different between us and someone else. Have you ever admired or envied someone so much you wished you *were* that person, or at the very least *just like* him or her? We can often get so far down the road comparing our lives to someone else's that we no longer feel comfortable in our own skin. We want to talk like that person, look like that person, act like that person, and live like that person.

I used to work with a guy who had a pretty sharp wit. One day a woman came in wearing an outfit that wasn't super flattering, and when this guy saw her, he said, "Somebody needs to tell her that just because it comes in your size doesn't mean it *fits* you!" Granted, it wasn't the nicest thing to say, but his words have stuck with me. Because you know what? It's so true. There's a world of difference between an outfit you buy off the rack and one that's been tailored specifically for your body. Likewise there *are* a host of other things I *could* do with my life. I could easily go work somewhere else or start a completely new career; I know I have the skills and abilities to, but that doesn't mean I'd be doing what God wants me to be doing. There's nothing worse than trying to wear something that doesn't fit you correctly. You feel awkward and uncomfortable until you're able to change. It's the same thing trying to be someone you're not!

I have to be comfortable being who He's made *me* to be. And you have to be comfortable being who He's made *you* to be. When we're willing to do that, that's when we'll have a truly satisfying contentment, peace, and happiness in our hearts and lives.

Now I know some of you have been wishing you could interject since the beginning of this chapter and say, "But wait! Isn't this all a bit lopsided? Comparison isn't *always* bad. What about the good kind of comparison?" And you'd be right. There *is* a good kind of comparison in addition to the bad.

Comparison *can* be good when it inspires you or encourages you to change by growing, maturing, and in any way becoming more like Jesus. The apostle Paul once said, "So imitate me, watch my ways, follow my example, just as I, too, always seek to imitate the Anointed One."[2] When you see someone who's following Jesus's example, it should encourage you to do so as well.

On the flip side, unhealthy comparison leaves you feeling defeated, ungrateful, critical, inadequate, prideful, or envious. And I believe it also completely stunts our spiritual and emotional growth.

Let's focus on the last element of that list for a bit—envy. When you envy someone else or their position in life, it cripples you from developing God's call in your own life and often leaves you feeling paralyzed. Trying to be somebody else and do what they do—when it's *not* what God's called *you* to do—will only lead to confusion and frustration in your life. The Bible tells us: "For where you have envy and selfish ambition, there you find disorder and every evil practice."[3] Being envious of someone else is like saying to God, "Yeah, I really don't like the way You created me. I kinda wish you'd made me *her*."

I tend to think in mental pictures. And as I was thinking about how comparison works, I got an image in my head of Noah's ark. Can you picture it in your head? A gigantic wooden boat floating on an endless sea carrying the world's only surviving humans and animals.

Now what if a wooden plank on the very bottom of the ark decided one day, "You know what? I'm sick of being down here where the sun doesn't shine. I don't feel like anybody appreciates me or all the hard work I'm doing. Nobody can even see what I'm doing! It's cold, it's wet, it's dark. That's it…I'm not doing this anymore. I'm gonna go up to the roof and trade places with one of the planks up there. Let's see one of *them* share in the sheer joy of being down at the bottom." And so the bottom plank pops herself off of the bottom of the ark and goes up on top.

When she finally reaches the top of the ark and everyone sees her, they all panic and ask, "Oh, no! What are you doing up here? This isn't where you belong. *Who's covering your spot right now?*" And the plank responds, "Calm down, y'all [since she's from the south side of the boat]! Stop freaking out. I'm just sick and tired of being at the bottom day in and day out. And I don't feel like y'all really appreciate what it takes to be down in the trenches all the time. So I decided I'm just gonna move myself on up!"

What would happen when that plank tried to be something she wasn't created to be? Water would start pouring into the ark from the bottom. The lower levels would flood. And the ark would begin to tilt and eventually sink. No more animals. No more people. And the plank would be left all by herself drifting aimlessly on the water for the rest of time.

I know that story's sort of silly, but isn't that exactly what we do? We decide we don't want to do what God's called us to do anymore; we want to be somewhere or somebody else. It inevitably leads to confusion and frustration and can set off a whole chain reaction of things in our lives, and everything is thrown off.

If my ark story didn't resonate with you, let me try one more illustration to drive home the point that comparison is totally insane. Have you ever seen or played with a Mrs. (or Mr.) Potato Head before? If you've no idea what I'm talking about, you are seriously missing out! Basically Mrs. Potato Head is a plastic toy in the shape of a potato with about ten or eleven holes in various spots so you can attach her plastic body parts— feet, arms, hair/hat, eyes, a mouth, nose, and ears. But imagine if you and I were built like Mrs. Potato Head and the different parts of our body could move around as they pleased.

So one day your feet say, "You know what? We're sick of being the feet and always having to be the ones to carry the weight. We just take everyone else everywhere they have to go. You stuff us into shoes; it's dark down here, and sometimes it even gets a little sweaty and smelly. We're not going to be feet anymore. We want to see the world, so we're gonna swap places with the eyes." What happens when your feet are firmly attached to the front of your face? They don't function the way they were designed to anymore, do they? And now, neither can your eyes. Right? Oh, the eyes can still see, but what good are they if all they can see is the inside of your socks?

I know it's just as silly as the ark story, but do you see how we do this to ourselves? *How we cripple ourselves by wanting to be someone different than who God's called us to be?*

Within our desire for something *we* consider better, we settle for less than what God clearly called "very good." We are created in *God's* image. You are His "VERY GOOD"! It simply doesn't get any better than that. Let's refuse to compare ourselves to others. It is wasting precious time that we could be spending on finding out who we are and why we were created. It's time to get on with living our lives for a higher purpose. You are amazing! It's time to believe that. Your family needs the real you full of life.

OK, so let's put on some trendy clothes, a little makeup, throw our hair in a ponytail, and walk our sassy little selves outside and live for Jesus. The world is looking for some life.

Chapter Twenty-Three

LABELS, LABELS, AND *MORE* LABELS

Your greatest comfort comes not from
what others think about you, but from
what God thinks about you in Christ—
forever loved, accepted, approved.[1]
TULLIAN TCHIVIDJIAN

A PLACE FOR EVERYTHING and everything in its place. I'm not going to lie—neat and tidy is the way to my heart. I don't love "organized chaos" like some of you may; I love "organized order." It's true, I'm a *huge* fan of organization. Can I get an amen? I experience tremendous joy and satisfaction when my home is neatly organized with everything in its specific place.

That's why I *love* my label maker, and I use it to label everything in my home. If you visited my house today, you'd quickly realize it's not perfect. But when you opened up the pantry, everything you saw would be neatly labeled. I have a breakfast bin labeled "breakfast." The baking bin is labeled…not to mention my baking spices and all of my cooking spices (in alphabetical order, of course). And then when you opened up my medicine cabinet, you'd see labels on our allergy medications, pain meds, stomach meds, and all of our various vitamins. That's just the way I like it—neatly organized in bins and accurately labeled.

Some people might say I'm crazy, but I'd just tell them that it's one of the unique ingredients God mixed into my personality. I firmly believe He's given me organizational skills, and I have to steward them well.

You may not know this, but every strength has a shadow side. It's what happens when the enemy gets in and distorts a strength or talent God has given us. Sometimes when we feel a loss of personal control in our lives, we seek to gain it back by controlling things and people around us. This includes compulsively deducing, diagnosing, summarizing, and *labeling* others along with ourselves. And I believe the dictionary defines that as judgment.

While labeling everything in my pantry and medicine cabinet is handy, the bad side of being in the habit of labeling everything is that I didn't even realize when I stopped labeling with truth and started labeling with lies.

I'd been labeling myself my entire life! And not

only that, I'd labeled everybody around me as well. If you didn't measure up according to my standards, you were "less than." When I didn't measure up to the women around me who I thought were amazing moms, I labeled myself "inadequate." When I had struggles in my marriage, I labeled myself "failure." When I couldn't afford to shop at name-brand stores, "cheap" was how I labeled my clothes and myself. When I was frustrated over how messy my house was, I was a "lousy house-keeper." When my friends' homes were decorated like something out of a *Southern Living* magazine, I labeled myself "inferior." When we couldn't afford a new car, I was "poor."

When I didn't know what to do with the hurt I'd buried deep inside from sexual abuse, I labeled myself "dirty," "afraid," "angry," "ashamed," "guilty," "unprotected."

When my sexual desires decreased after having children, I labeled myself "defective." When I felt like I didn't measure up spiritually or my faith wasn't as strong as my friends', I was "shallow." When I didn't feel as holy as those around me, I was "disqualified to share my story."

Have you ever labeled someone? Have you ever been labeled—whether by yourself or others? Labels like:

+ Rejected

+ Outcast

- Abandoned

- Betrayed

- Lonely

- Depressed

- Stupid

- Dumb

- Unloved

- Worthless

- Useless

- Ugly

- Anxious

- Jealous

- Insecure

It can be emotionally crippling to be labeled and feel like you can never change it.

Thankfully labels aren't permanent. They aren't the end of the story. They're actually removable.

The labels you've put on yourself or that others have put on you are removable because God, your loving Father, has the ability to peel off every one of those labels.

Never again do your circumstances or past events in your life have the power to label you and become your identity. God can pull them off or write over them with His truth.

So how do you break out of the terrible trap of comparison and experience the freedom that comes when God peels off your labels?

You start by declaring God's Word.

Realize that Satan doesn't have any new tricks. He tries to ensnare us using the same tactics he used on Eve. We need to determine that we're not going to keep falling into his traps and start refuting his lies and accusations with truth. If you've placed your trust in Christ and are His disciple, you can stand firm on the promises of God's Word.

I believe one of the reasons why I love to label things is because God is a labeler too. God is the Author of labels, and when *He* types and attaches a label on you, it's always life-giving and points back to Him.

When you feel defeated, God says, "You're more than a conqueror."[2] When you feel worthless, God says, "You're precious and honored in My sight, and I love you."[3] When you feel that you don't measure up in your appearance, God says, "I knit you together before you were even born; you're fearfully and wonderfully made."[4]

Start declaring *God's* labels over yourself:

+ Conqueror

+ Confident

+ Pure

+ Loved

+ Worthy

+ Successful

+ Chosen

+ Brave

+ Champion

You are beyond compare, friend. Ask God to whisper in your heart *His* label for you. Ask Him to remove the old labels of false comparison, judgments, fear, insecurity, and inferiority. And then ask Him for the grace and courage to walk in the joy and freedom of who He says you are today and always.

Chapter Twenty-Four

AND THE STORY
GOES ON...

For them it was only the beginning of the
real story. All their life in this world had
only been the cover and title page: now at
last they were beginning Chapter One of
the Great Story which no one on earth has
read: which goes on forever: in which every
chapter is better than the one before.[1]
C. S. LEWIS

SO HERE WE are. We've gone on a journey together
over the past twenty-three chapters, and now we've
arrived here at the end of the book.

We sincerely hope you've learned some valuable
truths you can apply in your life going forward. And
more importantly, our prayer is that you heard the

Holy Spirit's voice speaking to you and showing you His will for your story.

But even though we've reached the end of the book, this is not the end of the story—for me or for you. This is just the start of a new exciting scene in the script.

Now you get to wake up every morning and make a choice: "Am *I* going to write my story today? Or am I going to surrender my pen to God and let *Him* be the Author of my story?"

And watch; when you make the choice day in and day out to live out the script God has written for your story, you'll be blown away by how amazing His plans for you are.

But God doesn't make our stories amazing solely for our own enjoyment and entertain. As we talked about in chapter 18, there's a *much* bigger picture.

Your story is about so much more than just your life. It doesn't stand in isolation on its own.

Your story, my story, the stories of women and men all around the world who've surrendered their pens to God and are letting Him write on their pages…all of them are being woven together like the threads of gorgeous tapestry to create a magnificent masterpiece— one great eternal story that grows larger and larger as more and more new threads continue to be added and woven through.

I love how N. T. Wright describes the part our individual stories play in the larger, more cosmic story:

What you do in the present—by painting, preaching, singing, sewing, praying, teaching, building hospitals, digging wells, campaigning for justice, writing poems, caring for the needy, loving your neighbor as yourself—will last into God's future.[2]

Your story doesn't begin and end with your life here on earth. When you let God be the Author, He weaves it into something bigger...a story that leaves a legacy.

Doesn't that sound exciting? I don't know about you, but when I die, I want to leave a lasting legacy for my children and my children's children and on and on for generations.

And we do that by living out stories—our lives—carrying God's love wherever we go. Rick Warren says:

Love leaves a legacy. How you treated other people, not your wealth or accomplishments, is the most enduring impact you can leave on earth.[3]

Do you want to leave a legacy? Then love. Let your life be marked by the kind of extravagant, selfless, sacrificial love that marked Jesus's life:

We are surrounded by a great cloud of people whose lives tell us what faith means. So let us run the race that is before us and never give up. We should remove from our lives anything that would get in the way and the sin that so easily holds us back. Let us look only to Jesus, the One who began our faith and who makes it perfect.[4]

Follow *His* example. And in turn, as you follow Him, your story will inspire, motivate, encourage, and be an example for others watching *your* life.

And forever your story goes on.

NOTES

Introduction | Before We Begin . . .

1. C. S. Lewis, *The Horse and His Boy* (New York: HarperCollins Publishers, 1954), 165.

Chapter One | Blank Page

1. Twitter.com, Karen Kingsbury tweet, https://twitter.com/KarenKingsbury/status/358413268475330560 (accessed March 20, 2014).
2. Hebrews 11:6.

Chapter Two | Masterpiece

1. Hannah Goodwyn, "Steven Curtis Chapman Looks to *The Glorious Unfolding*," CBN Music, http://www.cbn.com/cbnmusic/interviews/steven-curtis-chapman-glorious-unfolding-goodwyn.aspx (accessed March 20, 2014).
2. As quoted in AnnaMaria Andriotis, "10 Things the Beauty Industry Won't Tell You," MarketWatch.com, April 20, 2011, http://www.marketwatch.com/story/10-things-the-beauty-industry-wont-tell-you-1303249279432 (accessed March 20, 2014).
3. Amazon.com, Self-Help Books, http://www.amazon.com/books-used-books-textbooks/b/ref=sa_menu_bo?ie=UTF8&node=283155 (accessed March 20, 2014).
4. Genesis 2:18, NAS, emphasis added.
5. Genesis 2:22, NAS.
6. Genesis 1:27, NIV.
7. Numbers 23:19; Deuteronomy 4:15–16; John 4:24.

8. Eric D. Naus, "God's Feminine Attributes" (blog), MoodyChurch.org, July 12, 2011, http://www .moodychurch.org/crossroads/blog/gods-feminine -attributes/ (accessed March 20, 2014). Institute for Creation Research, http://www.icr.org/article/6776/

9. Genesis 2:25, The Voice.

Chapter Three | Focus

1. Charles Swindoll, *Jesus: The Greatest Life of All* (Nashville: Thomas Nelson, 2009), 255.

2. Genesis 3:1–7, niv, emphasis added.

3. 2 Corinthians 10:12, The Voice.

4. PreventBlindness.org, "Vision Problems in the U.S.," http://www.visionproblemsus.org/ (accessed March 20, 2014); David Dunaway and Ian Berger, "World-wide Distribution of Visual Refractive Errors and What to Expect at a Particular Location," presentation to the International Society for Geographic and Epidemiologic Society. Preview available at Scribd.com, http://www.scribd.com/doc/161680442/ Worldwide-Distribution-of-Visual-Refractive-Error1 (accessed March 20, 2014).

5. Genesis 3:7, niv.

6. Genesis 3:8–11, niv, emphasis added.

7. 2 Corinthians 5:7, esv.

8. 2 Corinthians 5:7, The Voice.

9. Matthew 7:11.

10. Isaiah 63:1.

11. Philippians 4:19.

12. Philippians 4:7.

13. 1 John 4:8.

14. 1 John 4:18, ncv.

15. Psalm 34:4, esv.

16. Ephesians 1:17–19, The Message, emphasis added.

17. 1 Peter 2:4–6, esv, emphasis added.

Chapter Four | What's in a Name?

1. Twitter.com, Beth Moore tweet, https://twitter
   .com/BethMooreLPM/status/433231447659253760
   (accessed March 20, 2014).
2. Ira Rosofsky, "Was Shakespeare Wrong?—Would a
   Rose by Any Other Name Smell as Sweet?", *Adventures in Old Age* (blog), PsychologyToday.com, January 11, 2010, http://www.psychologytoday.com/
   blog/adventures-in-old-age/201001/was-shakespeare
   -wrong-would-rose-any-other-name-smell-sweet
   (accessed March 20, 2014).
3. Amazon.com, Baby Names, http://tinyurl.com/
   mvhzj4d (accessed March 20, 2014).
4. Laura Wattenberg, "Obsessed With Baby Names?
   You're Not Alone," *The Blog* (blog), HuffingtonPost
   .com, April 10, 2013, http://www.huffingtonpost
   .com/laura-wattenberg/obsessed-with-baby-names-_
   b_3038990.html (accessed March 20, 2014).
5. Genesis 21:6.
6. Genesis 25:25–26.
7. Exodus 2:10.
8. Genesis 5:2, kjv, emphasis added.
9. Genesis 2:24.
10. Genesis 2:23, nlt.
11. Genesis 3:20, nlt.
12. Revelation 2:17, niv, emphasis added.
13. Isaiah 62:2–4, nlt, emphasis added.

CHAPTER FIVE | DON'T STOP BELIEVING

1. Brennan Manning, *Abba's Child: The Cry of the Heart for Intimate Belonging* (Colorado Springs: NavPress, 1994, 2002), 60.
2. Genesis 3:20, NLT.
3. Genesis 11:4–9, NIV, emphasis added.
4. Judges 9.
5. John 6:28–29, NCV, emphasis added.
6. Colossians 3:10, NLT.
7. Romans 10:11, ESV.

SECTION 2 | THE TRUTH ABOUT GUILT

1. QuoteInvestigator.com, "I Would Rather Walk With a Friend in the Dark Than Alone in the Light," May 10, 2013, http://quoteinvestigator.com/2013/05/10/walk-with-friend/ (accessed March 20, 2014).

CHAPTER SIX | LET IT GO!

1. Joyce Meyer, "Seven Ways to Waste Your Time," CP Living, March 9, 2010, http://www.christianpost.com/news/seven-ways-to-waste-your-time-44202/ (accessed March 20, 2014).
2. I, Adana, have firsthand knowledge of this survey through partnering with Beth Moore's ministry several years ago.
3. See Proverbs 22:6.
4. Isaiah 6:1–3, NIV.
5. See Isaiah 6:5.
6. Isaiah 6:6–7, NCV.
7. Genesis 15:17–18; 19:24; Exodus 3:2–5; 13:21; Malachi 3:2; Acts 2:1–4; Hebrews 12:29; Revelation 20:9–10.
8. 1 John 1:9, THE VOICE.

CHAPTER SEVEN | CHOSEN

1. Twitter.com, Jon Acuff tweet, https://twitter.com/JonAcuff/status/300597258951467009 (accessed March 20, 2014).
2. Ephesians 1:4–5, NLT, emphasis added.
3. Galatians 4:4–7, NLT, emphasis added.
4. Romans 8:14–17, NLT, emphasis added.
5. Hebrews 10:22, NLT, emphasis added.
6. Max Lucado, *Max on Life: Answers and Insights to Your Most Important Questions* (Nashville: Thomas Nelson, 2010), as quoted on GoodReads.com, http://www.goodreads.com/quotes/412940-when-grace-moves-in-guilt-moves-out (accessed March 20, 2014).
7. John 10:10, THE MESSAGE.

CHAPTER EIGHT | DISCOVERING YOUR RHYTHM

1. BrainyQuote.com, "Jean Nidetch Quotes," http://www.brainyquote.com/quotes/quotes/j/jeannidetc143976.html (accessed March 20, 2014).
2. Micah 7:7–8, NLT.
3. See Psalm 118:24.

CHAPTER NINE | AN ANCHOR YOU CAN CLING TO

1. Elisabeth Elliot, *A Chance to Die: The Life and Legacy of Amy Carmichael* (Ada, Michigan: Revell, 2005), 223, as quoted in Danielle Lee, "Amy," *Stay the Course* (blog), January 24, 2014, http://www.staythecourseblog.com/2014/01/amy.html (accessed March 21, 2014).
2. Exodus 3:11–14, NLT.

CHAPTER TEN | YOU CHOOSE

1. William Jennings Bryan, "America's Mission," speech delivered by the leader of the Democratic Party at the Washington Day banquet given by the Virginia Democratic Association at Washington DC, February 22, 1899, as quoted in Thomas B. Reed, ed., *Modern Eloquence Part One* (Whitefish, MT: Kessinger Publishing, LLC, 2005), 95.
2. Job 1:1–3, 13–20.
3. Job 2:7–10.
4. Hebrews 10:23, THE MESSAGE, emphasis added.
5. 1 Thessalonians 5:23, THE MESSAGE, emphasis added.
6. Deuteronomy 30:19–20, NLT, emphasis added.

CHAPTER ELEVEN | SMALL FAITH, A BIG MOUTH, AND A GOOD GOD

1. Blaise Pascal, *Thoughts* 4.248, as viewed at Bartleby .com, "Section IV: Of the Means of Belief," http:// www.bartleby.com/48/1/4.html (accessed March 21, 2014).
2. Matthew 17:20, THE VOICE.

CHAPTER TWELVE | BEING COURAGEOUS IN CONFLICT

1. Robert McKee, *Story: Substance, Structure, Style, and the Principles of Screenwriting* (New York: HarperCollins Publishers, Inc., 1997), 210.
2. Max Lucado, *When God Whispers Your Name* (Dallas: Word Publishing, 1994), 44.

Chapter Thirteen | The Art of Peace

1. Larry Crabb, *Becoming a True Spiritual Community: A Profound Vision of What the Church Can Be* (Nashville: Thomas Nelson Publishers, 2007).
2. Psalm 133:1, GW.
3. Psalm 139:23–24, The Voice.
4. Daniel Goleman, *Emotional Intelligence: Why It Matters More Than IQ* (New York: Bantam Books, 1995), 43.
5. Proverbs 3:5–6, The Message.
6. Proverbs 15:22, NIV.
7. Gary Smalley, *The DNA of Relationships* (Carol Stream, IL: Tyndale House Publishers, 2005), 169.
8. Matthew 22:37–39, NIV, emphasis added.
9. Ephesians 4:15, NIV, emphasis added.

Chapter Fourteen | Pause

1. Brené Brown, "Wishing You Love and Light" (blog), December 18, 2012, http://brenebrown.com/2012/ 12/18/20121218wishing-you-love-and-light-html/ (accessed March 21, 2014).
2. Genesis 16:1–6, NLT.
3. Genesis 17:3–7, 15–21, NLT.
4. Genesis 21:1–3, NLT.

Chapter Fifteen | Vantage Point

1. C. S. Lewis, *The Magician's Nephew* (New York: Harper Collins Publishers, 1955), 136.

Chapter Sixteen | Amnesia

1. Twitter.com, Bob Goff tweet, https://twitter.com/ bobgoff/status/367360659236724737 (accessed March 21, 2014).

CHAPTER SEVENTEEN | ASSUME NOTHING

1. Caroline Leaf, *Switch on Your Brain: The Key to Peak Happiness, Thinking, and Health* (Ada, MI: Baker Books, 2013), 133–134.
2. Psalm 66:5, NCV.
3. Isaiah 64:4, NIV.
4. Romans 8:28, NIV.
5. Corrie ten Boom, John Sherrill, and Elizabeth Sherrill, *The Hiding Place*, 35th anniversary edition (Grand Rapids, MI: Chosen Books, 2006), 12.

CHAPTER EIGHTEEN | TUNNEL VISION

1. Frances Hodgson Burnett, *The Secret Garden*, 1910 as quoted on GoodReads.com, http://www.goodreads.com/quotes/49472-if-you-look-the-right-way-you-can-see-that (accessed March 21, 2014).

CHAPTER NINETEEN | BETTER TOGETHER

1. Wayne Cordeiro, *Leading on Empty: Refilling Your Tank and Renewing Your Passion* (Grand Rapids, MI: Bethany House Publishers, 2010), 71.
2. James 5:16, NIV.

CHAPTER TWENTY | SUPERNATURAL PERSPECTIVE

1. Robert Morris, "Open Your Spiritual Eyes," *It Is Written*, Day 22, Gateway Devotions, http://gatewaydevotions.com/it-is-written/day-22 (accessed March 21, 2014).
2. Galatians 6:4–5, NCV, emphasis added.
3. Psalm 103:8–14, NIV.
4. Deuteronomy 7:9, NLT.
5. Psalm 40:5, NLT.

6. Hebrews 4:12, NLT.
7. 2 Peter 1:3, NLT.

CHAPTER TWENTY-ONE | NO WIN IN COMPARISON

1. Andy Stanley, The Comparison Trap sermon series, 2012, http://northpoint.org/messages/comparison-trap (accessed March 21, 2014).
2. Genesis 3:4–5.
3. Genesis 3:11, NLT.
4. 2 Corinthians 10:12, NLT.

CHAPTER TWENTY-TWO | TAILOR MADE

1. Christine Caine, Lifetime Journey, ChristineCaine.com, http://www.christinecaine.com/content/life time-journey/gjenyf (accessed March 21, 2014).
2. 1 Corinthians 11:1, THE VOICE.
3. James 3:16, NIV.

CHAPTER TWENTY-THREE | LABELS, LABELS, AND MORE LABELS

1. Twitter.com, Pastor Tullian tweet, https://twitter.com/PastorTullian/status/2376902002085888 (accessed March 21, 2014).
2. Romans 8:37.
3. Isaiah 43:4.
4. Psalm 139:13–14.

CHAPTER TWENTY-FOUR | AND THE STORY GOES ON…

1. C. S. Lewis, *The Last Battle* (New York: Harper-Collins Publishers, 1956), 210–211.
2. N. T. Wright, *Surprised by Hope* (New York: HarperCollins Publishers, 2008), 193.

3. Rick Warren, *The Purpose-Driven Life* (Grand Rapids, MI: Zondervan, 2002), 125.
4. Hebrews 12:1–2, NCV.